FAILED TRANSITION, BLEAK FUTURE?

FAILED TRANSITION, BLEAK FUTURE?

War and Instability in Central Asia and the Caucasus

Hooman Peimani

Westport, Connecticut
London

Library of Congress Cataloging-in-Publication Data

Peimani, Hooman, 1957–
   Failed transition, bleak future? : war and instability in Central Asia and
the Caucasus / Hooman Peimani
      p.   cm.
   Includes bibliographical references and index.
   ISBN 0–275–97504–5 (alk. paper)
   1. Asia, Central—History—1991–   2. Transcaucasia—History—20th
century.   I. Title.
DK859.5.P45   2002
958'.04'3—dc21   2001054586

British Library Cataloguing in Publication Data is available.

Library of Congress Catalog Card Number: 2001054586
ISBN: 0–275–97504–5

First published in 2002

Praeger Publishers, 88 Post Road West, Westport, CT 06881
An imprint of Greenwood Publishing Group, Inc.
www.praeger.com

Printed in the United States of America

The paper used in this book complies with the
Permanent Paper Standard issued by the National
Information Standards Organization (Z39.48–1984).

10 9 8 7 6 5 4 3 2 1

To my son Justin

Contents

List of Tables

FAILED TRANSITION,
BLEAK FUTURE?

1

Introduction

The collapse of the Soviet Union and the emergence of the new states in the Caucasus and Central Asia in late 1991 created a hope among their peoples for a future different from their dissatisfactory past. The new era offered an opportunity for democracy and prosperity to those people who had lived under various forms of undemocratic regimes for about two centuries. It also provided grounds for optimism about peace and political stability in the entire Eurasia—that is, the region consisting of all the countries around and in close proximity to the Caspian Sea, connecting Asia to Europe. Instability in that region could potentially destabilize two continents housing six of the seven declared nuclear states: China, France, India, Pakistan, Russia, and the United Kingdom. The disintegration of the Soviet Union initiated a process of transition from a failing Soviet system built on a command economy to a hoped-for democratic one based on a type of free-enterprise economy. Besides limited and/or superficial successes, the economic development record since independence of almost all the ex-Soviet republics has been disappointing, if not disastrous. In particular, the transitional process has only increased the political, economic, and social difficulties of the Caucasian countries and the Central Asian (hereafter CA) countries while being unable to ensure their achievement of the desired new societies. Both "poor" (Armenia and Georgia in the Caucasus; Kyrgyzstan and Tajikistan in Central

Asia) and "rich" (Azerbaijan in the Caucusus; Kazakhstan, Turkmenistan, and Uzbekistan in Central Asia) countries have failed to establish even the basic foundations of such societies a decade after their independence. They are all in an economic limbo. This means that their economies are neither socialist nor capitalist, but contain all the negative characteristics of the two economic systems without having most of their benefits. It goes without saying that there are differences among these countries in terms of their degree of progress in dealing with their immediate challenges and achieving their long-term objectives. Nevertheless, they all suffer from a wide range of shortcomings inherited from the Soviet era as well as those that have emerged since the fall of the Soviet Union.

In spite of their differences in terms of area, population, and mineral and energy resources and their degree of achievements since independence, there has been a prevailing negative trend in all the Caucasian and CA countries. It has been evident in their worsening political, economic, and social situations. Their ruling elites have been unable to address their numerous and ever-increasing problems. Without exception, they have all established highly centralized and undemocratic political systems in their respective countries. The salient characteristic of their authoritarian polity has been a zero-tolerance policy toward any meaningful political dissent. Without a doubt, authoritarianism has been a means for ensuring the interests of the Caucasian and CA ruling elites concerned about the loss of their preeminent status in the postindependence era. Apart from that, authoritarianism has been their response to the worsening situation and to the rising political and social dissent in their countries which threatens their national security and stability. It has also been their reaction to the emerging instability in parts of their countries or in those of their neighbors while reflecting their concern about destabilizing forces in certain countries in their close proximity—namely, China, Russia, and Afghanistan.

If the existing negative trend continues, the entire Caucasus and Central Asia will likely head toward long-term tension and instability. The first and foremost victims of this undesirable future will obviously be the three Caucasian and five CA countries. Yet, this bleak future will also have major implications for a number of regional (Iran, China, Turkey, and Russia) and nonregional (United States) powers with long-term interests in the two regions most of which share borders with them. The deteriorating situation will create a suitable ground for the emergence and growth of political extremism among the peoples of the Caucasus and Central Asia, who are mostly dissatisfied with the status quo. These frustrated and disenchanted peoples will likely find the extremist political ideologies and programs more appealing and more convincing than those of their discredited rulers. The latter's legitimacy is being questioned by a growing number of their nationals for a wide range of reasons, including incompetence, rampant corruption, and an antidemocratic style of government.

In response to the rising internal threat, the ruling elites will likely resort to nationalism. In particular, they might promote extreme forms of nationalism, including chauvinism, as experienced in many other countries in different continents confronting the same situation. Creating an appealing alternative to that of the opposition extremist groups aimed at the dissatisfied people will be one of its major objectives. Extreme nationalism will be very attractive for the youth—the social stratum most vulnerable to extremist ideologies and the main targets of extremist groups. The ruling elites might also find their resort to extreme nationalism necessary for the sake of consolidating their challenged power apparatus. In this case, they could seek to manipulate the nationalist sentiment of their peoples as a means to increase their legitimacy and strengthen their social basis of support. However, using the nationalist card will have a negative backlash, with weakening and destabilizing effects on its users. Extreme nationalism could, and will likely, provoke ethnic conflicts within the multiethnic Caucasian and CA countries. It could therefore lead to civil wars. Moreover, it could spread fear in the neighboring countries. They might feel threatened by the surge of nationalism in their vicinity, which could easily take the form of expansionism in the Caucasian and CA countries characterized with territorial and border disputes.

In addition to various external influences, many internal social, economic, and political factors will determine in what form and to what extent instability will surface in each Caucasian and CA country. Needless to say, based on the specific situation in each country there will be differences in its shape and in the extent of its initial emergence. Regardless of these differences, the logical and predictable outcome of the current trend will likely be instability in the form of civil, interstate, and regional wars in the Caucasus and Central Asia. The existence of unsettled, although currently inactive, violent conflicts (i.e., independence movements and civil wars) in these two regions have left no doubt about the feasibility of this scenario. To this list, one should also add the existence of many ethnic grievances and territorial and border disagreements, which will likely create a suitable ground for the instigation of new ethnic conflicts and territorial disputes in violent forms. For a number of reasons, there is a great possibility that many of them could escalate to civil wars and interstate wars, respectively. Among other factors, the ethnic makeup of the Caucasus and Central Asia and the existence of many sources of conflict between their regional states will pave the way for their further escalation to the level of regional wars, despite the intention of their initiators.

The presence of certain regional (Iran, China, Turkey, and Russia) and nonregional (United States) powers with long-term interests in the two regions will have a certain impact on the development of the scenarios mentioned above and will likely contribute to the extent, intensity, and duration of wars of various forms. In particular, the presence of these powers will increase the possibility of their intentional or unintentional involvement in those wars in support of one side or another, while preserving their interests. Depending on the situation, whether this involvement takes a direct or indirect form will be determined by many factors, including the importance of the affected Caucasian or CA countries for each of the five states and the latter's political, economic, and military capabilities. These factors also include the geographical realities, which, depending on the case, facilitate or impede their access to the affected countries, and the overall political environment in Central Asia and the Caucasus. The latter determines whether a foreign intervention in whatever form can take place at all. The possibility of some or all of the five states being dragged into any future military conflict will therefore strengthen the potential for the escalation and expansion of military conflicts in either of the two regions. War and instability in these energy-producing regions bordering regional and global powers with strong conventional military and/or nuclear capabilities will have long-term political, economic, and security implications. They will not be confined only to the countries directly involved in any future regional military conflict. In one way or another, they could affect the stability of the Caucasus and Central Asia as well as that of the Asian and/or European regions in their proximity. As a result, wars in whatever form in those two regions could escalate and affect the stability of the international system and global peace.

In developing the main argument of this book, chapter 2 provides a general overview of the situation in the Caucasian and CA countries at the time of independence. It also deals with the various existing political, economic, and social influences in terms of their importance to the current situation. The inherited problems of the Soviet era shared by all the former Soviet republics are given special attention with regard to their long-term implications on the development of these countries. However, the problems specific to these countries are also discussed in detail.

Chapter 3 offers an account of the general situation in the Caucasian and CA countries a decade after their independence. In particular, it elaborates on their failure to address the pressing political, economic, and social difficulties inherited from the Soviet era over the decade following their independence. The chapter also deals with specific post-Soviet era problems of importance to the economic and social development of the Caucasian and CA countries and to their long-term stability.

Chapter 4 analyzes the internal and external factors responsible for the emergence of authoritarianism in virtually all the Caucasian and CA countries. In this regard, authoritarianism is discussed as an effort by the elites in those countries to strengthen their political systems in reaction to the growing internal instability. Therefore, authoritarianism is approached as a logical consequence of the worsening internal situation and the rise of dissent in different forms in these politically fragile countries. The chapter also deals with the emergence of extremism in various forms among the dissatisfied regional peoples. To that end, a number of factors contributing to this phenomenon are discussed. The promotion of nationalism, especially in its extremist form, by the regional elites as a response to political extremism of the emerging opposition groups receives special attention. Moreover, the chapter evaluates the impact of the rising dissent and instability in the Caucasus and Central Asia or in the countries in their proximity (Afghanistan, China, and Russia) on the growth of extremism and nationalism.

Chapter 5 concentrates on the factors contributing to the rise and expansion of instability in these two regions in the forms of civil, interstate, and regional wars. To that end, the chapter studies various feasible scenarios under which such conflicts could take place, while dealing with the influences determining their extent, intensity, and duration. It also sheds light on the possibility of further escalation as a result of the intentional or unintentional engagement of certain regional (Iran, China, Turkey, and Russia) and nonregional (United States) powers. In its treatment of the factors forming their interests in the Caucasian and/or CA countries, this chapter offers an analysis of different feasible and predictable circumstances under which these powers could be dragged into wars involving one or a group of the mentioned countries. It also studies various influences that might facilitate or hamper their engagement in such wars.

Chapter 6 concludes the main argument of this book. It sums up the major findings while offering an account of the regional and international impact of various forms of instability in the Caucasus and Central Asia. It also suggests certain feasible efforts on the part of regional and nonregional states which could enable the Caucasian and CA countries and their neighbors to avoid long-term instability or prevent its escalation should such efforts fail.

2

General Overview of the Caucasian and the Central Asian Countries at the Time of Independence

BASIC DATA ON THE COUNTRIES OF THE CAUCASUS AND CENTRAL ASIA

The Caucasus and Central Asia are part of Eurasia, a region consisting also of Iran and Russia. The first two regions are connected via the Caspian Sea, which is the largest lake in the world with no link to any open sea. The Caucasus borders Russia to the north and the northeast, Iran to the south, the Caspian Sea to the east, and the Black Sea and Turkey to the west. Three former Soviet republics—Azerbaijan, Armenia, and Georgia—form this region, all of which gained independence in 1991 when the Soviet Union collapsed. Through its ports on the Black Sea—Supsa, Bhutumi, and Sukhumi—Georgia provides access to international waters for all three Caucasian countries.

Based on the latest available official statistics of 1998, the populations of Azerbaijan, Armenia, and Georgia are about 7.7 million, 3.5 million, and 5.1 million, respectively.[1] However, these statistics do not take into consideration the compulsory displacement of people through wars and ethnic tensions. Nor do they account for the voluntary migration of people since independence. In particular, the official statistics of Azerbaijan and Armenia are no longer valid because of the forcible displacement of large numbers of Azeris and Armenians, respectively. The Azeri-Armenian military conflict (1988–94) over Nagorno Karabakh forced over one million Azeris residing in the territory and also in Armenia to leave for Azerbaijan's territories outside the war-affected areas during the years of the conflict. Similarly, the ethnic conflict between the Azeris and the Armenians made the Armenian residents of Azerbaijan leave that country for Armenia in the same period. As a result, there are now large numbers of refugees in both countries. Additionally, many regional people have left the Caucasus for Russia and non-CIS (Commonwealth of Independent States) countries in search of peace and/or employment. The number of economic migrants has been especially large in the case of Armenia, as according to the official estimates between 800,000 and 1,500,000 of its citizens have left the country since independence.[2] As a result, the available official statistics are somewhat misleading, although it is clear that all the Caucasian countries have small populations and their numbers have been decreasing. Azerbaijan, Armenia, and Georgia are also small in area—respectively 86,600 square kilometers, 29,800 square kilometers, and 69,700 square kilometers.

Central Asia is a land-locked region neighboring four countries. It shares borders with Russia to the north and the northwest, Iran and Afghanistan to the south, the Caspian Sea to the west, and China to the east. The region comprises the former Soviet republics of Kazakhstan, Kyrgyzstan, Tajikistan, Turkmenistan, and Uzbekistan, which emerged as independent states in 1991. Based on 1998 statistics, their population are 16.3 million, 4.6 million, 6 million, 4.3 million, and 23.6 million, respectively.[3] Kazakhstan is the largest CA country at 2.7 million square kilometers. Kyrgyzstan, Tajikistan, Turkmenistan, and Uzbekistan are 199,000, 143,000, 488,000, and 447,000 square kilometers, respectively.

THE CAUCASIAN AND THE CENTRAL ASIAN COUNTRIES AT THE TIME OF INDEPENDENCE

Independence in 1991 came as a surprise to the eight Soviet republics in the Caucasus and Central Asia. This was especially true for the CA republics, which were the least enthusiastic proponents of the dissolution of the Soviet Union. There were no significant pro-independence movements in the Caucasian and CA republics during the last few years of the Soviet Union, a time when such movements were flourishing elsewhere in that country. Independence movements emerged in Georgia and, to a lesser extent, in Azerbaijan toward the end of the Soviet Union, but they were not as extensive or as popular as those of the Baltic republics and the Ukraine.[4] However, the lack of enthusiasm for acquiring statehood status in the Caucasian and CA republics was not a sign of their satisfaction with the status quo. Rather, it reflected the heavy dependence of these Asian Soviet republics for their survival on the Soviet Central government in Moscow. As the most underdeveloped and poorest Soviet republics, they were the least prepared to function as independent states. Their appreciation of this fact diminished their desire for independence.

At the time of independence in 1991, the Caucasian and CA states encountered a variety of economic challenges. The fall of the Soviet Union had been preceded by a decade of poor economic performance affecting all aspects of life in that country. The Soviet economy began to experience major problems in the 1960s, which became worse in the 1970s and 1980s. In particular, the state-dominated economy was in deep trouble in the last decade of the Soviet Union, and this provided the economic ground for its fall. The depth of the economic problems and their clear worsening trend forced the Soviet leaders to express concern about the situation, thus breaking with their traditional policy of denying that any problems existed in their country. The rise of Mikhail Gorbachev to the highest position in the Soviet system—that is, the general secretary of the Communist Party—demonstrated the Soviet elite's appreciation of the intensity of the expanding economic and social difficulties. It also showed their understanding of the need to address these difficulties to prevent the fall of their political system.

Mikhail Gorbachev unsuccessfully tried to solve the numerous problems of his country through his envisaged comprehensive political and economic reforms. Aiming at rejuvenating the Soviet system, he sought to address all its problems without touching its very foundation. As the latter was the core cause of most of its shortcomings, this objective turned his reforms into a mission impossible. In a comparative sense, he was more successful in implementing his political reforms. The intention of these was to open the closed Soviet political environment, which was intolerant of any type of expression of views and activities other than those sanctioned by the Soviet Communist Party. Those reforms did not turn the Soviet Union into a democracy, but they certainly loosened strict political and social restrictions on the Soviet people. As for the economic reforms, the Gorbachev reforms were, without a doubt, failures. Not only did they not stop the Soviet economic decline, they worsened all the economic problems and pushed the ailing Soviet economy further into trouble. As a result, the Soviet economy was suffering from major problems in 1991 when the Soviet Union fell.

Without exception, all the economic sectors (i.e., agriculture, industry, and services) were experiencing extensive difficulties that made them unable to meet fully the basic needs of their country. In particular, the chaos in the agricultural and industrial sectors hampered their normal function and resulted in a severe decline in the production and availability of products all over the country. According to the last available official Soviet statistics, covering the first nine months of 1991, the Soviet economy experienced a sharp decline in all aspects of its activities. The decline was clearly reflected in negative rates in major economic indicators—for example, GNP, –12%; industrial production, –6.5%; agricultural production, –10%; oil production, –9%; coal production, –11%; and foreign trade, –38%.[5] In addition to severe shortages of goods as a result of the economic decline, closures of state-owned industrial and agricultural facilities, growing unemployment, and rising prices worsened the situation. To this picture, one should add a three-digit and rising inflation rate, a large foreign debt estimated at $80 billion, and low foreign-exchange reserves.[6]

Consequently, the leaders of the 15 Soviet republics inherited a troubled economy upon independence in late 1991. It was simply incapable of meeting the basic needs of their populations. As will be discussed, the newly independent states of the Caucasus and Central Asia faced certain economic difficulties peculiar to their countries in addition to those common to all Soviet republics. These made their situation exceptionally difficult, imposing a formidable challenge on their unprepared leaders and populations alike.

Major Challenges at the Time of Independence: Politics, Economy, and Ethnicity

Politics

The 1991 collapse of the Soviet Union led to the independence of the three Caucasian and five CA countries. The Russian Empire conquered and annexed the entire Caucasus during two series of long wars with Iran—the empire that had previously ruled over the region—in the late eighteenth century and the early nineteenth century. The first of these wars led to the loss of most parts of the Caucasus, as recognized by Iran in the treaty of Golestan of 1813.[7] Iran lost the remainder in another series of wars that began a few years later. The Turkmenchai Treaty of 1828 finalized the separation of the entire Caucasus from Iran and put that region under Russia's sovereignty.[8] The fall of the Czarist Russia in February 1917 and the Bolshevik Revolution of October 1917 provided the opportunity for a short-lived independence of the Caucasian countries. Right after the fall of Czarist Russia, the Armenians, the Azeris, and the Georgians established a joint Caucasian republic named the Caucasian Commissariat. This multiethnic republic survived until early 1918, when each Caucasian ethnic group opted for establishing its own state.[9] Armenia established its independent Republic of Armenia and Georgia formed the Georgian Democratic Republic, both of which lasted for a short while until 1921. Azerbaijan established the Mussavat Republic, named after its forming party, which continued until 1920. Over a three-year period, the Bolshevik forces engaged in bloody wars with the three republican forces, leading to their suppression between 1920 and 1921. The Soviet Union had fully restored Moscow's power over the three Caucasian countries by 1921.[10] The Caucasus remained part of the Soviet Union until the latter's collapse in 1991. The recognition of the independence of the Caucasian countries by the Russian state in Moscow ended their two-century subjugation to the Russian and Soviet states. Under the Russian and Soviet regimes, the borders of the three countries changed several times until the region gained its current political geography in the 1930s. The redrawing of borders based on political considerations, rather than on social and historical realities, planted the seeds of ethnic conflicts. The ongoing Azeri–Armenian territorial dispute over Nagorno Karabakh is a well-known example of this situation.

Russia occupied and annexed Central Asia gradually over a two-century process. War and, to a lesser extent, diplomacy helped the Russians expand their control over the region. The process began in the second half of the eighteenth century and was completed about a decade before the start of the twentieth century. During this lengthy process, the administrative structure of the region was changed several times. In its final form, the Kazakh-dominated area was integrated into the Russian Empire as one political and geographical entity, Kazakhstan, and the rest as another, Turkestan. World War I and the Bolshevik Revolution did not bring independence to the annexed region, though they did change its traditional structure. The dissatisfaction of the Central Asians with the exploitative Russian system took the form of many anti-Russian, anti-Soviet, independence movements during 1916–33. The Soviet regime suppressed them all brutally.[11] The Soviets kept the regional boundaries of Central Asia but did not keep its pre–World War I structure. They divided and redivided that region several times until 1936, when it was finally divided into five so-called ethnically based republics. Each republic was named after its numerically strongest ethnic group. As an assurance of their docility, each republic ended up with large minorities of CA origin, a recipe for internal ethnic conflict with obvious destabilizing political and social effects. Among other factors, the existence of almost all the CA ethnic groups in every regional country has provided a situation conducive to the expansion of one country's ethnic tension—and therefore political instability in various forms—to other regional countries. Through this elaborate scheme, the Soviet regime made efforts at independence by each CA republic a very risky gamble. Given the ethnic structure of the CA republics, such a move would have opened doors to the rise of opposition or nationalist movements among the ethnic minorities of any CA republic aspiring to independence from the Soviet Union.

The three Caucasian and the five CA republics were part of the highly centralized Soviet political and economic system. The Soviet central government in Moscow determined, designed, and controlled the political, economic, and social lives of these republics through central planning. Like other Soviet republics, they simply implemented the economic, political, and social policies as determined by the Soviet central planners. As part of a Soviet-wide division of economic, political, and military activities among the Soviet republics, each Caucasian and CA republic had to perform certain predetermined tasks to ensure the normal function of the Soviet Union. The Caucasian and CA political, economic, social, and military structures were therefore developed to perform the designated duties. This made them functional as components of a large political system. Consequently, they became unable to run most of their republican affairs without the heavy assistance of the Soviet central government, in the forms of cash, equipment, machinery, raw material, and fuel. In short, all the political, economic, and military institutions of these republics were designed to provide for the needs of the Soviet Union without regard to their own specific local needs. To implement the centrally designated plans, their political apparatuses were developed as branches of the Soviet central government designed to represent and preserve Soviet interests. As they were appointed by the Soviet government in Moscow, their leaders had only limited powers of decision-making, confined to those aspects of political, economic, and social affairs with no bearing on the centrally planned policies. As branches of the Soviet central government, the Caucasian and CA governments were established and run as highly centralized political entities.

Economy

The Soviet regime kept the entire Caucasus and Central Asia underdeveloped and less prosperous in comparison to the European part of the USSR.[12] In a relative sense, the three Caucasian republics were more advanced and prosperous than the five CA republics, although they were still far behind the Soviet Slavic republics (Russia, Ukraine, and Belarus). Central Asia was the least industrialized and the poorest region of the Soviet Union. Two years before the fall of the Soviet Union, more than 33% of the entire CA population fell below the poverty line, in comparison to 5% and 7% of the population of Russia and the rest of the USSR, respectively.[13] Without doubt, there were differences among the Caucasian republics and also among the CA republics in terms of richness, natural resources, industrial advancement, and military capabilities. In a broad sense, Armenia, Georgia, Kyrgyzstan, and Tajikistan were "poor" and the least blessed with natural resources, while the rest were "rich" with significant natural resources such as fossil fuel, mainly oil and natural gas. Within the same context, the Caucasian countries were more industrialized than the CA ones, while Azerbaijan, Kazakhstan, and Uzbekistan were the most industrialized countries of the two regions. Despite these differences, all the Caucasian and CA countries were more or less on the same footing at the time of independence, even though the "richer" ones were more hopeful for a rapid economic recovery and a more prosperous future.

All eight Caucasian and CA countries faced more or less the same general pattern of challenges and opportunities at the time of independence in 1991. There were at least five major challenges.

1. For most of their needs, the countries of the Caucasus and Central Asia depended on other parts of the Soviet Union. In particular, they depended heavily on Russia for just about every necessity, including industrial products, spare parts, consumer goods, medicine, food products, and fuel. The Soviet government supplied them with these items and cash to help them meet the needs of their populations. Hence, they all required Russian assistance for their normal functioning. When the Soviet Union collapsed, the sudden withdrawal of this assistance further aggravated their economic problems and paralyzed their weak economies. They had to stand on their own at a time when they were experiencing severe shortages of cash, budget deficits, and financial problems—all the "natural" results of losing Russian assistance. The sudden loss was a devastating blow to all the Caucasian and the CA countries. It was particularly devastating for the latter because of their heavy dependence on ex-Soviet central government assistance. The depth of dependence on Moscow at the time of independence was clearly evident in, for example, Tajikistan's reliance on Russia for 80% of its fuel and 75% of its foodstuffs.[14] Another example is Uzbekistan, which received 6.4 billion rubles from Moscow in 1990, equal to 43% of its total expenditures in that year.[15] In the year of independence (1991), Uzbekistan was the largest beneficiary of Soviet assistance in the Soviet Union, amounting to 19.5% of its GDP.[16]

Given their heavy dependency on the centrally provided assistance in cash and kind, the collapse of the USSR and independence severely shook the economic institutions of all the Caucasian and CA countries. As their republics had been developed to address the agricultural and, to a lesser extent, energy needs of the USSR, their industrial sector was the least developed.[17] Moscow imposed single-product agriculture on Azerbaijan and the CA republics by using their fertile land mainly for cotton production for the Russian textile industry and for exports. Cotton was one of the major hard-currency-earning Soviet exports. The heavy emphasis on cotton, under both the Russian and Soviet regimes, led to a sharp increase in land under cotton cultivation at the expense of farming land for food production. Between 1913 and 1986, the phenomenal increase of this from 648,000 hectares to

7,100,000 hectares made Central Asia the largest cotton producer of the Soviet Union, totalling about 90% of Soviet annual cotton production.[18] However, the massive allocation of resources to cotton production made Azerbaijan and Central Asia dependent on Russia and other Soviet republics for other agricultural products, such as foodstuffs. This dependency also existed for Armenia and Georgia, whose domestic products were inadequate due to the underdevelopment of their agriculture. The depth of dependency on foreign sources for foodstuffs was quite evident in Turkmenistan, for instance, in 1992, a year after independence: it imported two-thirds of its grain needs, almost half of its milk and dairy-product requirements, and all of its sugar.[19] Heavy emphasis on cotton production also created an environmental disaster in Kazakhstan and Uzbekistan, which might subsequently affect other CA countries, in the form of the rapid drying of the Aral Sea and the contamination of its water supplies and also of the land in its proximity. The result has been the devastation of the economy of a large area around the Aral Sea where about three million people live.[20]

In essence, the situation was not very different in the Caucasus. In a relative sense, the Caucasian republics had more advanced and more diversified economies, but they still depended heavily on Russia and other Soviet republics for most of their agricultural and industrial needs.[21] Unlike Kyrgyzstan, Tajikistan, and Turkmenistan, Azerbaijan, Armenia, and Georgia had had relatively significant industrial sectors as the industrialization of their region began in the nineteenth century, a century before Central Asia embarked along that road. Their agricultural sectors were more developed than most CA republics in terms of food production, but they were still far short of self-sufficiency. Despite their relative advancement compared to most CA republics, the Caucasian republics were unable to produce their essential agricultural and industrial needs. Like their CA counterparts, they had to depend on Russia and other Soviet republics to satisfy most of those needs. For example, in 1989, Georgia had to import 25% of its electricity, almost all its fuel and gas, over 80% of its timber, about 50% of its cement, and almost 90% of the raw materials used in its light industry.[22] It also had to import 60% of its dairy products, over 50% of its grain, and over one-third of its meat.[23]

Heavy dependency on Soviet assistance and on Russia created serious shortages of various products immediately after independence.

The collapse of the Soviet system, which heavily damaged the pillars of the command economy such as governmental planning and management, resulted in chaos in the production and distribution systems of goods produced in all eight Caucasian and CA countries. This development aggravated the shortages of essential items, including food and fuel[24] caused by the sudden cessation of Soviet assistance, and led to skyrocketing prices. Right after independence, prices jumped severalfold all over the former Soviet republics, including in the Caucasian and CA countries. Price increases were especially high in Central Asia, a region with extensive dependency on assistance from Moscow. This was a "natural" result of massive shortages of essential goods previously supplied by the latter. The increases were on average sixfold in Uzbekistan,[25] more than tenfold in Kazakhstan,[26] and twelvefold in Tajikistan.[27] Price increases were much larger for certain products in very short supply such as fuel, which rose about twentyfold in Kyrgyzstan.[28]

2. The industrial sectors of the Caucasian and CA countries had major deficiencies. They were weak, irrelevant to their immediate needs, outdated, and/or heavily dependent on Russia for spare parts and/or market. All these countries had some industries, but their economic role in the Soviet Union as the producers of nonindustrial goods limited their industrialization. Despite differences in terms of extent and diversification, their industries were much weaker than the Slavic part of the Soviet Union. In Central Asia, Kyrgyzstan, Tajikistan, and Turkmenistan had very insignificant industries, which were mainly related to their main economic activities: agriculture and mineral extraction.[29] Kyrgyzstan's industries were not even able to process its major products—wool, cotton, and tobacco.[30] Kazakhstan and Uzbekistan had more advanced industries, including heavy industries such as military equipment, metallurgy, and energy.[31] However, they lacked light and consumer industries to meet their immediate requirements, while their heavy industrial products were mainly irrelevant to their needs. Kazakhstan, for instance, although unable to produce food products, had the capability for the production of transporters and launchers for missiles and also the production of military aircraft.[32] Uzbekistan could produce advanced fighter jets such as the MIG-29 and military transport aircraft—for example, the IL-76.[33] Most of these two countries' industries were outdated and in need of extensive

investments for upgrading and/or expansion. Uzbekistan's oil industry, which required large funds to become self-sufficient, serves as an example.[34]

Compared to most of their CA counterparts, the Caucasian republics were more industrialized, but their industries were mainly unrelated to their immediate needs. As was the case in Central Asia, they were established to address certain needs of the USSR as a whole, which required their production of certain products in demand in other parts of the USSR. Azerbaijan was the most industrialized regional country, but its industries were mostly oil-related, lacking many other essential ones.[35] Being about a century and a half old, its oil industry was more advanced than those of Turkmenistan, Kazakhstan, and Uzbekistan, most of which emerged in the second half of the twentieth century. The Georgian and Armenian industries—consisting of heavy industries such as advanced military hardware production (e.g., military aircraft)—were small and incapable of producing most of their necessities.[36]

Finally, the Caucasian and CA industries were heavily dependent on Russia for spare parts, expertise, funding, and markets. Lack or shortage of funds and/or spare parts pushed many operational economic units to closure. In the absence of Russia's market, low-quality Caucasian and CA products, like those of all other former Soviet republics, could not be sold easily in markets elsewhere. In general, the Caucasian and CA industries were underdeveloped and lacked viable light-industry, consumer, and high-tech branches, in addition to their heavy dependency on Russia for other reasons.

3. As a result of their designated role in the Soviet economy, the Caucasian and CA countries had types of exports and imports that reflected their economic underdevelopment. By and large, they all exported to other regions of the Soviet Union nonindustrial and unprocessed products—namely, raw materials, minerals, oil and natural gas, and certain agricultural products (mostly cotton). They mainly imported industrial goods and foodstuffs from those regions. For example, even though it was one of their most industrialized countries, Uzbekistan's main export in 1991 was cotton, accounting for 84% of its total exports.[37]

4. The Caucasian and CA economies contained several major problems, including very high inflation and unemployment, rising prices,

and shortages of various goods for private and commercial consumption. Beginning in the 1980s, a significant decline in virtually all the sectors of their economies (agriculture, industry, and services) was responsible for all these economic ills. The economic reforms of the Gorbachev era (1985–91) increased their problems by adding new ones such as rising unemployment, inflation, and closure of factories. For example, a year after independence the inflation rate was 1,200% in Azerbaijan and 1,540% in Kazakhstan, reflecting the prevailing situation in their respective regions.[38]

5. All the Caucasian and CA countries were unable to meet their energy requirements through their own resources, irrespective of their differences in terms of the availability of energy reserves in their territories. As a result, they were dependent on each other and/or on Russia for oil, natural gas, and coal. In general, they both exported and imported oil, natural gas, coal, and/or electricity. This strange pattern was a result of their lack of sufficient energy resources or the underdevelopment of their energy industries. In the Caucasus, Azerbaijan had extensive oil and gas resources, but they were not fully developed.[39] In particular, its natural gas reserves were mainly underdeveloped making it dependent on Russian gas, while its oil refineries were completely dependent on Russian spare parts. Armenia lacked significant energy resources, while Georgia had limited and mainly undeveloped oil reserves, which can meet only a fraction of its needs. As a result, they both relied on Azerbaijan for oil and Russia for natural gas.[40]

In Central Asia, the situation was not fundamentally different. Kazakhstan had the largest energy resources of the region. It was especially rich in oil, but its natural gas and coal deposits were also substantial. However, these resources were mainly underdeveloped. Hence the Kazakhs had to import natural gas from Uzbekistan and crude oil from Russia.[41] Uzbekistan had enough resources of oil and natural gas, although mainly underdeveloped, to become self-sufficient, and it was a major producer of electricity.[42] The Uzbeks exported natural gas to neighboring Kazakhstan, Kyrgyzstan, and Tajikistan, but they imported crude oil and oil products from Russia.[43] Kyrgyzstan and Tajikistan were not self-sufficient in energy resources, although they did have small deposits of oil, natural gas, and coal; however, these were adequate to meet only a small portion of their needs, forcing them to import the rest from their neighbors and Russia.[44]

Facing certainly formidable challenges, the Caucasian and CA countries also faced potential opportunities. They all had certain economic advantages, which, if fully developed, could help them meet at least some of their short- and long-term needs. The Caucasus had significant deposits of nonferrous metals, hydrocarbons (oil and natural gas), coal, and building materials. Metallic ores such as iron, copper, and molybdenum ores existed in large quantities in the region. For example, Azerbaijan and Georgia were rich in iron and manganese, respectively.[45] While not fully industrialized, Armenia, Azerbaijan, and Georgia had a relatively significant industry as well as a large number of scientific personnel. The latter could help their countries embark on industrial development to make them self-sufficient or to meet at least some of their industrial needs as well as those of their regional and/or neighboring countries. The Caucasus had the potential to develop its agriculture, which was mainly producing fruits and vegetables. The Caucasians could not only aim at meeting their food requirements, they could also seek to generate income through the export of certain products such as cotton. In fact, the Azeris were a major cotton-producer in the Soviet era and were able to continue their exports.

Central Asia was rich in mineral resources and fossil energy (oil and natural gas), while having an extensive cotton production. For example, Kyrgyzstan was rich in precious metals, including gold. Turkmenistan had extensive on-shore and off-shore natural-gas reserves in addition to significant oil deposits. Kazakhstan had large on-shore and off-shore oil reserves. Tajikistan was a cotton producer and could expand its cotton cultivation to generate revenues in hard currencies through exports. Turkmenistan and Uzbekistan were major cotton-producers, producing over 90% of the Soviet cotton production.[46] They were the main cotton exporters in the Soviet era and could count on their continued exports as a substantial source of revenue in foreign currencies. Despite their shortcomings, the industries of Kazakhstan and Uzbekistan could satisfy some of their needs and help their economic growth, while meeting part of the demands of other regional countries. Thus, the existence of different potentials and capabilities created hope among the Caucasians and Central Asians that they could overcome their transitional difficulties and embark on development projects to address their immediate needs and future requirements.

Ethnicity

There is a dominant ethnic group in each Caucasian and CA country, after which that country is named. In the Caucasus, Azeri, Armenians, and Georgians account for 71%, 93.3%, 69% of Azerbaijan, Armenia, and Georgia, respectively.[47] In Central Asia, Kazakhs, Kyrgyz, Tajiks, Turkmen, and Uzbeks form about 50%, 52%, 63%, 72%, and 71% of their countries' populations—Kazakhstan, Kyrgyzstan, Tajikistan, Turkmenistan, and Uzbekistan, respectively.[48] Yet each country has large numbers of other regional ethnic groups and Slavs—mainly Russians and to a lesser extent Ukrainians—who form large minority communities. As a nonregional ethnic group, Russians have numerically strong communities in the CA countries. At the time of independence, their largest communities were in Kazakhstan and Kyrgyzstan, where they accounted for 38% and 22% of their populations, respectively.[49] In other CA countries, they formed small communities accounting for 7.6% (Tajikistan), 8% (Uzbekistan), and 9.5% (Turkmenistan) of their respective population.[50] The Russians constituted small communities in the Caucasus, accounting for 1.5% of Armenia's population and about 6% of the population of Azerbaijan and Georgia each.[51] In all the eight countries, minorities whose kin dominate one regional country form strong communities. There are also many small communities of other ethnic groups, such as Iranians and Lezgins in Azerbaijan, Ossetians and Abkazs in Georgia, Kurds and Greeks in Armenia, Tatars in all CA countries, Germans and Uyghurs in Kazakhstan and Kyrgyzstan, and Jews in Azerbaijan, Tajikistan, and Uzbekistan.

Having ethnic links with other countries in their respective region, the existence of large regional ethnic groups in each Caucasian and CA country has planted the seeds of ethnic tensions, including civil wars. It has also ensured that the rise of nationalism or ethnic conflict of one sort or another in one regional country can easily spread over the whole of the region. At the time of independence, this peculiar social characteristic made the ruling elites of the newly independent states in the Caucasus and CA concerned about the vulnerability of their respective countries as well as their regions to internally or externally provoked ethnic conflicts. The ethnic link among the three Caucasian countries and among the five CA countries made it clear to their rulers that, at best, it would be extremely difficult to achieve or maintain stability in one country if its neighbors were unstable. Undoubtedly, any major ethnic movement in the Caucasus or Central Asia would have dire political consequences for that region and for its constituent countries.

NOTES

1. UNDP, *Human Development Report 2000* (New York: Oxford University Press, 2000), 224.

2. "Brain Drain in Armenia," Institute for War & Peace Reporting (IWPR), Caucasus Reporting Service, 10 Jan 2000, 08:44:04 EST.

3. *Human Development Report 2000*, 224–225.

4. For an account on the rise of ethnic movements in different republics of the Soviet Union, see Ben Eklof, *Soviet Briefing: Gorbachev and the Reform Period* (Boulder, CO: Westview Press, 1989), 147–167.

5. "Europe: The End of an Empire," *Strategic Survey 1991–1992* (May 2000), 27.

6. Ibid.

7. Bahram Amirahmadian, "The Trend of Developments in the Karabakh Crisis," *Majelieh-e Motaellat-e Asyaie Markazi va Ghafghaz [Central Asia and the Caucasus Review]* (Tehran), 28 (Winter 2000), 32.

8. Ibid.

9. Kaveh Bayat, "A Look at the Relations of Iran with the First Armenian Republic, 1918–1921," *Majelieh-e Motaellat-e Asyaie Markazi va Ghafghaz [Central Asia and the Caucasus Review]* (Tehran), 25 (Spring 1999), 128.

10. Ibid.

11. For details, see Helene Carrere d'Encausse, "The Fall of the Czarist Empire," in *Central Asia: 120 Years of Russian Rule*, ed. Edward Allworth (Durham, NC: Duke University Press, 1989), 207–223; Helene Carrere d'Encausse, "Civil War and New Governments," in *Central Asia: 120 Years of Russian Rule*, ed. Edward Allworth (Durham, NC: Duke University Press, 1989), 224–253.

12. Matha Brill Olcott, "Central Asia's Political Crisis," in *Russia's Muslim Frontier,* ed. Dale F. Eickelman (Bloomington, IN: Indiana University Press, 1993), 54.

13. Jane Falkingham, Jeni Klugman, Sheila Marine, and John Micklewright, "Household Welfare in Central Asia: An Introduction to the Issues," in *Household Welfare in Central Asia*, ed. Jane Falkingham, Jeni Klugman, Sheila Marine, and John Micklewright (London: Macmillan, 1997), 1.

14. *Seeds of Change: Survival in the Pamirs.* Video produced by the Aga Khan Foundation, 1995.

15. *Republic of Uzbekistan.* Report of a UNICEF/WHO Collaborative Mission with the Participation of UNDP, UNFPA and WFP (21 February to 2 March 1992), Tashkent, Uzbekistan, 16 March 1992, 4.

16. UNDP, *Development Cooperation: Uzbekistan* (New York: UNDP, June 1995), 7.

17. Sohrab Shahabi, "A General View of the Economic Conditions of CA Republics," *Majelieh-e Motaellat-e Asyaie Markazi va Ghafghaz [Central Asia and the Caucasus Review]* (Tehran), 1, No. 2 (Autumn 1992), 122–123; Nasrin Nosrat, "The Economic Situation of the Republic of Azerbaijan," *Majelieh-e Motaellat-e Asyaie Markazi va Ghafghaz [Central Asia and the Caucasus Review]* (Tehran), 1, No. 3 (Winter 1994), 84, 86.

18. Ibid., 120–121.

19. Nassrin Nossrat, "The Economic Situation of the Republic of Uzbekistan," *Majelieh-e Motaellat-e Asyaie Markazi va Ghafghaz [Central Asia and the Caucasus Review]* (Tehran), 1, No. 4 (Spring 1993), 239.

20. For details, see: Michael Fergus, "The Aral Sea Environmental Crisis: Problems and a Way Forward," *Asian Affairs,* 30, No. 1 (February 1999), 35–44; Max Spoor, "The Aral Sea Basin Crisis: Transition and Environment in Former Soviet Central Asia," *Development and Change*, 29, No. 3 (July 1998), 409–435.

21. A. M. Ivanov, "Armenia's Economic Co-operation with Russia," *Majelieh-e Motaellat-e Asyaie Markazi va Ghafghaz [Central Asia and the Caucasus Review]* (Tehran), 28 (Winter 2000), 128.

22. Institute for War & Peace Reporting, Caucasus Reporting Service, No. 15b, Mon 24 Jan 2000, 07:24:20 EST.

23. Ibid.

24. *The Invisible Emergency: A Crisis of Children and Women in Tajikistan,* Report of a UNICEF/WHO Collaborative Mission with the Participation of UNDP, UNFPA and WFP (17–21 February 1992), 13; *The Looming Crisis of Children and Women in Kyrgyzstan*, Report of a UNICEF/WHO Collaborative Mission with the Participation of UNDP, UNFPA, WFP, 21–26 February 1992 (17 March 1992), 5; *Independent Republic of Kazakhstan,* Report of a UNICEFIWHO Collaborative Mission with the Participation of UNDP, UNFP, 4 and WFP (17–26 February 1992), Alma Ata, Kazakhstan, 17–26 February 1992, 13.

25. *Republic of Uzbekistan*, 4.

26. *Independent Republic of Kazakhstan*, 13.

27. *The Invisible Emergency*, 13

28. *The Looming Crisis of Children and Women in Kyrgyzstan*, 5.

29. "General Economic Outlooks and Prospects," *DEIK Bulletin-Kyrgyzstan* (Istanbul) (April 1993), 2; "Tajikistan: Introductory Survey," in *The Europa World Year Book 1994* (London: Europa Publications, 1994), 2752.

30. "The Economy," *DEIK Bulletin-Kyrgyzstan* (Istanbul) (June 1994), 2.

31. Nossrat, "Economic Situation of Uzbekistan," 238; Shahabi, "General View," 19.

32. Hooman Peimani, *Regional Security and the Future of Central Asia: The Competition of Iran, Turkey, and Russia* (Westport, CT: Praeger, 1998), 69.

33. Ibid.

34. Nossrat, "Economic Situation of Uzbekistan," 238.

35. For an account on Azerbaijan's oil industry and its significance for its economy, see: Mohammad Sarir and Narsi Ghorban, "Developments of the Oil Industry in Azerbaijan and Its Regional and International Positions," *Majelieh-e Motaellat-e Asyaie Markazi va Ghafghaz* [*Central Asia and the Caucasus Review*] (Tehran), 2, No. 1 (Summer 1993), 169–184.

36. Ivanov, "Armenia's Economic Co-operation," 128.

37. Ibid., 239.

38. Roland Dannreuther, "Creating New States in Central Asia," *Adelphi Paper* 288 (March 1994), 35.

39. For details, see Sarir and Ghorban, "Developments of the Oil Industry," 169–184.

40. Ibid., 183–184.

41. Kazakhstan's import was very significant in 1995, for instance. See "Tajikistan: Introductory Survey," in *The Europa World Year Book 1994* (London: Europa Publications, 1994), 2752.

42. "Economic Outlooks and Prospects: Natural Resources," *DEIK Bulletin-Uzbekistan* (Istanbul) (April 1993), 2.

43. Roland Dannreuther, "Creating New States in Central Asia," *Adelphi Paper 288* (March 1994), 22.

44. Peimani, *Regional Security and the Future of Central Asia*, 93; "The Economy: Energy," *DEIK Bulletin-Kyrgyzstan* (Istanbul) (June 1994), 2.

45. Mohammad Salmasi-zadeh, " A Glance at the Historical Geography of Georgia. From the First Century to the End of the 10th Century," *Majelieh-e Motaellat-e Asyaie Markazi va Ghafghaz* [*Central Asia and the Caucasus Review*] (Tehran), 28 (Winter 2000), 106.

46. Shahabi, "General View," 121–122.

47. Institute for War & Peace Reporting, *TransCaucasus: A Chronology*, 9, No. 6 (June 2000), 1.

48. Peimani, *Regional Security and the Future of Central Asia*, 43.

49. Ibid.

50. Ibid.

51. IWRP, *TransCaucasus: A Chronology*, 1.

3

Overall Situation in the Caucasus and Central Asia a Decade after Independence

When it comes to political and economic development, the post-independence record of the Caucasian and Central Asian countries has been one of disappointment. Without exception, all these countries, like other ex-Soviet republics (with the partial exception of Estonia), have experienced a very difficult time. Their postindependence era has been characterized by a declining economy and rising political and social problems, although their extent and intensity have varied from one country to another. The hope shared by both their peoples and their leaders that the enormous difficulties of the independence era would be only a passing phenomenon and that all these countries would soon initiate a more prosperous life has proven to be unrealistic. A decade after independence, the overall situation in the Caucasian and CA countries is not only not improving, it is in many respects worsening. The passage of time has made it clear to most, if not all, the Caucasians and the Central Asians that their hopes for an improvement in their lives may not be fulfilled for an unpredictably long time. The worsening economic, political, and social situations in their countries have made this point evident. A brief analysis of the prevailing situation in the Caucasus and Central Asia a decade after independence should substantiate this statement.

ECONOMIC SITUATION

Without exception, independence devastated the economies of all the Caucasian and CA countries and shook their social fabric. In particular, the paralysis of their economies not only created severe economic problems (high inflation, skyrocketing prices, shortages, etc.), but also paved the way for a weakening of their social order corresponding to that of the preindependence economic system. The sudden collapse of the Soviet system severely damaged the already troubled economies of these newly independent countries, which were incapable of meeting the basic needs of their respective peoples. Major shortcomings (e.g., chronic shortages, low-quality products, and inefficient industries and agriculture) were the main features of the Soviet economy worsened by the Gorbachev reforms. The ex-Soviet republics, including those of the Caucasus and Central Asia, inherited this troubled economy at the time of independence. It is not surprising that all of them faced an enormous and increasing number of economic difficulties.

The fall of the Soviet Union led to a sudden collapse of the highly centralized and state-dominated Soviet economy. In turn, the collapse initiated a transitional period from a command economy to a type of free-enterprise economy at a time when none of the 15 independent states was prepared for it. Not surprisingly, the result was a sudden shock to their economies. In the absence of a viable new economic system, the dismantling of the command economy worsened all the inherited economic shortcomings. Massive closure of state enterprises in the urban and rural areas created high unemployment and a large decline in the production of industrial and agricultural goods. This situation, coupled with the collapse of the Soviet distribution system, further worsened the chronic shortage of basic products, including foodstuffs, that had been a major characteristic of the Soviet economy. As a result of lack or shortage of fuel and/or spare parts, frequent power, water, and natural-gas cuts disrupted the daily lives of people and harmed industrial and agricultural production, resulting in lower output. This situation created shortages and reduced exports. The latter contributed to the deterioration of the financial situation of the former Soviet republics, as they had already lost their share of Soviet assistance in cash. Moreover, the sudden cut in interrepublic trade and economic cooperation between and among the ex-Soviet republics further worsened the economic situation in the Caucasian and CA countries.

Facing a new reality, the Caucasian and CA republics, like all other former Soviet republics, opted for restructuring of their economies. They initiated economic reforms to replace the crumbling socialist economies with a type of free-enterprise economy through decentralization and creation of a strong private sector. This reform was a necessity both for addressing their economic problems and for creating an economic foundation for their newly independent states. It was quite clear to all of them that political independence would be meaningless and unsustainable in the absence of a viable and growing economy. Hence, political and economic motivations demanded an overhaul of the Soviet-created republican economies. In practice, all the Caucasian and CA leaders have come to the realization that the establishment of a new economic system in absence of adequate domestic resources and substantial foreign assistance (e.g., loans, grants, and equipment) is a Herculean task. Two major factors have slowed down the transitional process in their countries, if not stopped it completely. One has been the lack of required resources—human, raw material, machinery, equipment, and funds. Another has been the fear of a sudden eruption of political dissent as a result of radical, sudden, and therefore painful economic reforms. Predictably, these reforms would lead to massive unemployment, sharp lowering of living standards, and widespread poverty, at least in the short run. With a few exceptions such as Estonia, all the former Soviet republics, including those of the Caucasus and Central Asia, have chosen to keep major aspects of the Soviet economy while encouraging a limited degree of free enterprise. The emerging market economy has been mainly confined to the service industry and small-scale industrial and agricultural enterprises.

The Caucasian and the Central Asian economies have all experienced serious difficulties in the postindependence period. Their industrial and agricultural production has sharply decreased as a result of a variety of factors, including the collapse of the command economy and central planning and the withdrawal of subsidies and transfers (cash, equipment, machinery, and fuel) from Moscow. They also include severe financial difficulties because of a lack of adequate domestic resources and a breakdown in interrepublic trade. As well, they include the inevitable consequences of the economic transition—for

TABLE 3.1   Percentage Annual GDP Growth in the Caucasus, 1993–2000

Year*	Azerbaijan	Armenia	Georgia
2000	7.5	5.5	6
1999	7.4	4.0	3.0
1998	10.0	7.2	2.9
1997	5.8	3.3	11.3
1996	1.3	5.8	10.5
1995	−11.8	6.9	2.4
1994	−19.7	5.4	−11.4
1993	−23.1	−14.8	−25.4

Source: Department of Economic and Social Affairs, *World Economic and Social Survey 2000* (New York: United Nations), 2000, 247.

* 2000 figures are estimates; 1999 figures are partly estimates.

example, price liberalization, privatization, and closure of nonviable enterprises. The economic decline is evident in the overall disappointing performance of all the Caucasian and CA economies during the first decade of independence (i.e., in the 1990s). This was reflected in their negative GDP growth rates throughout that period.

As is evident from Table 3.1, the economies of Azerbaijan, Armenia, and Georgia had contraction periods totalling, respectively, 54.6%, 14.8%, and 36.8% between 1993 and 2000. During that time, the expansion periods of the Azeri (32%) and of the Georgian (36.1%) economies were not large enough even to restore their strength at the time of independence, which was far below their needs. By contrast, Armenia's economy grew by 38.%, which enabled it to surpass its preindependence GDP strength by 23.3%. The impressive magnitude of this growth is somewhat misleading unless certain facts are taken into consideration. The extent of the underdevelopment of the country reflected in its economic shortcomings at the time of independence is one major fact. Suffice it to state here that the inability of the Soviet economy to meet the basic needs of the Soviet people was a main contributing factor to the demise of the Soviet Union. In the southern Soviet republics such as Armenia, economic underdevelopment was an additional problem. Hence, it will take several years, if not decades, of constant economic growth to address all the economic difficulties of

Armenia. One should also take into consideration the devastating economic impact of the Azeri–Armenian territorial dispute over Nagorno Karabakh. A ceasefire agreement ended that war in 1994, but both sides continued heavy defense expenditures in the 1990s, which was a large burden on their economies. In the case of Armenia, those expenditures offset to a significant extent the positive impact of its economic recovery and growth. For example, in 1998, military expenditure accounted for 3.6% of Armenia's GDP, which was almost double its expenditure on education of only 2% of its GDP.[1] The poor overall average growth rates for the period 1993–2000—that is, –2.8% for Azerbaijan, 2.91% for Armenia, and –0.09% for Georgia—demonstrate the disappointing economic performance of the Caucasian countries, despite the fluctuations in their annual growth rates.

In the case of the Central Asian countries, the economic decline was especially alarming in the 1990s. During 1993–2000, the economic performance of all the CA countries—including its two fossil-energy exporters, Kazakhstan and Turkmenistan—was disappointing, as demonstrated in Table 3.2. Hence, the economies of Kazakhstan, Kyrgyzstan, Tajikistan, Turkmenistan, and Uzbekistan had contraction periods totalling 31.9%, 48.5%, 46.8%, 56.4%, and 7.4%, respectively. With the exception of Uzbekistan, whose economic growth periods of 17.8% offset its shrinkage, the GDP growth rates in the

TABLE 3.2   Percentage Annual GDP Growth in Central Asia, 1993–2000

Year*	Kazakhstan	Kyrgyzstan	Tajikistan	Turkmenistan	Uzbekistan
2000	3.5	4	4	15	2.5
1999	1.7	2.2	3.7	16.0	4.1
1998	–1.9	2.1	5.3	5.0	4.4
1997	1.7	9.9	1.7	–11.4	5.2
1996	0.5	–7.1	–4.4	–8.0	1.6
1995	–8.2	–5.4	–12.5	–8.2	–0.9
1994	–12.6	–20	–18.9	–18.8	–4.2
1993	–9.2	–16	–11	–10.0	–2.3

Source: Department of Economic and Social Affairs, *World Economic and Social Survey 2000*. (New York: United Nations, 2000), 247.

*2000 figures are estimates; 1999 figures are partly estimates.

other countries fell far below their contraction rates. Accordingly, the economies of Kazakhstan, Kyrgyzstan, Tajikistan, and Turkmenistan had growth periods totalling 7.4%, 18.2%, 14.7%, and 36%, respectively. Consequently, all these economies experienced large negative average growth rates of –3.6% (Kazakhstan), –3.8% (Kyrgyzstan), –4% (Tajikistan), and –2.55% (Turkmenistan) between 1993 and 2000. Uzbekistan was the only economy with a positive average growth rate of 1.3%; although this is a sluggish rate, it reflects a significantly better economic performance in a comparative sense.

Years of consecutive negative growth rates have, to a large extent, led to the contraction of the Caucasian and the CA economies. If the current dismal growth rates continue, the gradual and low-rate positive economic growth will not compensate for the heavy damage of independence on the Caucasian and CA economies for a long time. One should also keep in consideration the fact that at the time of independence these economies were unable to meet most of the needs of their respective countries. In addition, they have all experienced population growth at a varying rate. Between 1990 and 1998, the population growth rate was 1.1% for Armenia, 1.4% for Azerbaijan, 0.4% for Georgia, 0.3% for Kazakhstan, 1.4% for Kyrgyzstan, 2.4% for Tajikistan, 2.8% for Turkmenistan, and 2.3% for Uzbekistan.[2] Given these two factors, the full recovery of their economies to the 1991 level will not be a real economic achievement for any of them. Their economies must grow substantially, probably by double-digit rates, for a long period of time, at least for a decade, to enable them to overcome all their major current shortcomings.

The Caucasian and CA economies have experienced a variety of difficulties since the collapse of the USSR. Of these, some are minor and are peculiar to one or another country, but there are six major difficulties shared by all of them.

1. The three Caucasian and five CA countries have failed to modernize, repair, and/or expand the necessary infrastructure. This is not to state that these countries have done nothing to address their infrastructural deficiencies. In fact, all of them have taken steps toward this end, but their achievements have been very limited. Thus, fully functional and adequate infrastructures are not yet in place. By and large, all the CA countries suffer from, for instance, inadequate transportation, telecommunication, and energy-production and -distribution systems. The severe fuel shortages in 2000 of the two so-called prosperous energy

producers and exporters—namely, Azerbaijan and Kazakhstan—gives an idea about the depth of the infrastructural problems in their respective regions. In that year, serious gas and oil shortages significantly decreased power production in Azerbaijan and compelled the Azeri government to increase its electricity imports from Iran.[3] In the same year, the shortage of oil for domestic consumption forced the Kazakh government to make the oil companies sell over 20% of their production intended for exports in the domestic market at low prices.[4]

2. The Caucasian and CA countries have not yet addressed their urgent industrial and agricultural constraints. They have largely failed to conduct the needed overhaul of their mainly outdated industries, significantly expand their industrial sector, and increase their industrial production and exports. As indicated in Tables 3.3 and 3.4, which cover the period 1990–98, for most of the 1990s all the Caucasian and CA countries experienced low or negative industrial and agricultural growth rates, which have continued to this date. Most of the newly built industries are small- and middle-sized, mainly producing light consumer goods. Recent examples include the establishment of a glass factory in Uzbekistan in 2000 and a tobacco factory in Kyrgyzstan in 2001.[5] In the cases of Georgia and Azerbaijan, the positive industrial growth rates are somewhat misleading. As with all industrial growth rates, many other economic activities in addition to manufacturing are included, such as construction. Various small construction projects (e.g., housing, shops, and restaurants) have been responsible for the positive rates. However, the growth of manufacturing, which is a necessity for long-term economic growth, has also been disappointing in these two countries. Between 1990 and 1998, its growth rate was negative in Azerbaijan (–6.1%) or very low in Georgia (0.7%).[6]

Beside industries, agricultural constraints still persist to a large extent. This is notwithstanding the fact that almost all the Caucasian and CA countries have increased their agricultural production or diversified their agriculture. A very impressive case is that of Tajikistan, whose food production was the lowest among the eight countries at the time of independence. Nevertheless, despite its efforts, it still has a very limited food production as its agriculture still focuses on cotton, which is a major or the major source of income and foreign currency respectively in Azerbaijan and most CA countries (Tajikistan, Turkmenistan, and Uzbekistan). Tajikistan has sought to diversify its agriculture and has limited cereal, fruit, and vegetable production, but it remains a food importer. It has made significant progress in increasing its grain production to over 500,000 tons in 1998, but it is still far from self-sufficiency as it requires between 300,000–500,000 tons of imported flour annually to meet its basic needs.[7] Contrary to the case of Tajikistan, that of Kazakhstan is a clear example of decline in food production in those Caucasian and CA countries with significant production capability prior to independence. It also demonstrates the deteriorating agricultural situation in all these countries in the post-independence era. Before independence, Kazakhstan had the most advanced and extensive agricultural sector in the entire non-European parts of the Soviet Union. However, since independence its food production has decreased significantly. For example, grain production declined from 21.6 million tons in 1993 to 12.3 million tons in 1997.[8] The production of other food items has also decreased significantly. Rice production fell from 480,000 tons in 1993 to 226,000 in 1996, potatoes from 2.29 million tons in 1993 to 1.67 million tons in 1996, and vegetables from 808,000 tons in 1993 to 778,000 in 1996.[9]

The Caucasian and CA countries have failed to draw up clear policies toward major issues affecting the development of their agricultural sectors. The most important issues are land ownership, land reform, the privatization of the state-owned farms, and the role of the state in agricultural production. Infrastructural restrictions, use of inefficient methods of production and outdated machinery, and lack of adequate investment have all contributed to the stagnation of agricultural sectors and to food shortages in almost all the Caucasian and CA countries. This has been reflected in negative agricultural growth rates in all these countries with the exception of Georgia, as evident in Tables 3.3 and 3.4.

3. All the Caucasian and CA countries have suffered from inadequate foreign financial assistance, whether in the form of aid packages or direct investments. Independence initiated a transitional period from the Soviet command economy to a market economy for which these countries were totally unprepared. Among other factors, they faced a major financial crisis, as their countries had insufficient financial reserves and no adequate domestic means for revenue generation. The public sectors were in a poor financial condition, but there was practically no significant or capable private sector to ease the financial burden. Nor did those countries receive a substantial amount of foreign financial assistance. Unlike other ex-Communist countries, for-

TABLE 3.3   Average Percentage Annual Agricultural and Industrial Growth in the Caucasus, 1990–98

Sector	Armenia	Azerbaijan	Georgia
Agriculture	–0.3	–1.4	5.5
Industry	–9.0	5.8	5.6

Source: The World Bank, *World Development Indicators 2000* (Washington, D.C.: The World Bank, 2000), 182.

eign investors and donors—in particular, Western ones—showed little interest in helping the former Asian republics of the Soviet Union. The bulk of foreign assistance went mainly to Eastern European countries, whose strength and independence from Russia seemed crucial for the security of the Western countries, in particular that of Western Europe. With respect to the former Soviet republics, Russia received the major part of foreign assistance, since instability as a result of the worsening economic situation seemed unacceptable for a country with a huge nuclear arsenal. The Caucasus and Central Asia have received a very limited amount of foreign assistance because of their limited economic significance for many Asian and Western investors and for their marginal security importance to many Asian and Western countries. Moreover, many investors did not want to involve themselves in a region with a high potential for inter-and intrastate conflict. In this regard, the growing instability in the Caucasus in the form of civil war in Georgia and Azerbaijan, together with the Armenian–Azeri dispute over Nagorno Karabakh, made that region a highly insecure place for investment. Even oil-rich Azerbaijan could not attract substantial for-

TABLE 3.4   Average Percentage Annual Agricultural and Industrial Growth in Central Asia, 1990–98

Sector	Kazakhstan	Kyrgyzstan	Tajikistan	Turkmenistan	Uzbekistan
Agriculture	–13.4	–1.2	–12.2	—	–1.0
Industry	–10.1	–12.0	–17.2	—	–5.1

Source: The World Bank, *World Development Indicators 2000* (Washington, D.C.: The World Bank, 2000), 183–184.

eign assistance except for its oil industry, dominated by Western oil companies. In Central Asia, Tajikistan was the only country suffering a civil war, but the possibility of the expansion of this war to other CA countries was another discouraging factor for investors. For Tajikistan itself, the civil war almost guaranteed no major foreign investment. In a relative sense, oil-producing Kazakhstan and militarily strong Uzbekistan received larger portions of the available amount of foreign assistance for Central Asia. Long-term political and economic considerations convinced foreign sources to funnel the larger share of their assistance to these countries. The exception has been Kyrgyzstan, which has received, in the form of aid, relatively large foreign assistance compared to other CA countries.

This pattern of foreign assistance (investment and aid) has persisted to this date. With respect to direct investment, Russia still receives far larger amounts than the Caucasian and CA countries. In 1998, for instance, the amount of direct investment in Russia was $2,183 million.[10] In the same year, the share of the eight Caucasian and CA countries was a fraction of that of Russia. The only exceptions were the two oil-producing countries, where various foreign oil companies—mainly American—made large investments. In 1998, the amount of foreign investment in Azerbaijan and Kazakhstan was $1,985 million and $1,158 million, respectively.[11] Yet the total average amount of investment in these two countries has been low, given their extensive energy resources. Azerbaijan, for instance, received $5 billion in investment during the period 1996 and 2000, making the average amount of annual investment about $1 billion.[12] Apart from the oil producers, the amount of foreign investment in the other six countries, including oil- and natural-gas-producing Turkmenistan, was very small in 1998. It was $251 million for Georgia, $232 million for Armenia, $102 million for Kyrgyzstan, $85 million for Uzbekistan, $80 million for Turkmenistan, and only $30 million for Tajikistan.[13]

In terms of aid, the amount of foreign assistance has also been very limited. As indicated in Tables 3.5 and 3.6, all eight Caucasian and CA countries have received negligible amounts of aid during the first two years of independence (1991 and 1992) and small amounts in 1997 and 1998. Even the share of foreign aid for oil and gas producers was insignificant, despite their importance for major Western economies whose oil companies have large stakes in their energy resources.

TABLE 3.5   Total Amount of Aid Received by the Caucasian States (U.S.$ millions)

Year	Azerbaijan	Armenia	Georgia
1998	88.7	138.5	162.4
1997	182	168	246
1992	5.6	22.5	5.3
1991	—	3	—

Source: UNDP, *Human Development Report 2000* (New York: Oxford University Press, 2000), 219–20; UNDP, *Human Development Report 1999* (New York: Oxford University Press, 1999), 194.

In the absence of generous foreign assistance, limited domestic resources have made the Caucasian and CA governments simply unable to meet the increasing financial requirements of their countries. The weakness of their private sectors, which lack the resources to share the financial burden, has made the situation especially difficult for their governments. They now have to meet all the financial needs of their countries, a mission impossible given their poor economic situation. Generally speaking, the increasing balance-of-payments deficits as indicated in their export–import imbalance (Tables 3.7 and 3.8) and their growing foreign debts (Tables 3.9 and 3.10) clearly reveal the inability of the Caucasian and CA governments in this regard.

TABLE 3.6   Total Amount of Aid Received by the Central Asian States (U.S.$ millions)

Year	Kazakhstan	Kyrgyzstan	Tajikistan	Turkmenistan	Uzbekistan
1998	207.1	216.1	105.1	16.6	144.3
1997	131	240	101	11	130
1992	9.5	3.5	11.7	5.4	1.4
1991	112	—	—	—	—

Source: UNDP, *Human Development Report 2000* (New York: Oxford University Press, 2000), 220; UNDP, *Human Development Report 1999* (New York: Oxford University Press, 1999), 196.

TABLE 3.7 Exports and Imports of the Caucasian Countries (U.S.$ millions)

Year	Armenia		Azerbaijan		Georgia	
	Export	Import	Export	Import	Export	Import
1998	360	988	1,010	2,425	720	1,437
1997	330	952	1,154	1,900	622	1,192
1996	368	888	757	1,443	479	798

Source: The World Bank, *World Development Indicators 2000* (Washington, D.C.: The World Bank, 2000), 244; The World Bank, *World Development Indicators 1999* (Washington, D.C.: The World Bank, 1999), 251; The World Bank, *World Development Indicators 1998* (Washington, D.C.: The World Bank, 1998), 234.

Table 3.8 Exports and Imports of the Central Asian Countries (U.S.$ millions)

Year	Kazakhstan		Kyrgyzstan		Tajikistan		Turkmenistan		Uzbekistan	
	Export	Import	Export	Import	Export	Import	Export	Import	Export	Import
1998	6,735	7,716	602	877	604	731	614	1,608	3,148	3,182
1997	7,611	8,279	676	817	807	801	759	1,004	3,980	4,417
1996	6,966	7,546	546	950	772	808	1,691	1,532	4,161	5,175

Source: The World Bank, *World Development Indicators 2000* (Washington, D.C.: The World Bank, 2000), 245–246; The World Bank, *World Development Indicators 1999* (Washington, D.C.: The World Bank, 1999), 251–252; The World Bank, *World Development Indicators 1998* (Washington, D.C.: The World Bank, 1998), 235–236.

TABLE 3.9   Growth in Burden of Debt in the Caucasian Countries (U.S.$ millions)

Year	Azerbaijan	Armenia	Georgia
1998	693	800	1,674
1997	504	666	1,446
1996	435	552	1,356

Source: The World Bank, *World Development Indicators 2000* (Washington, D.C.: The World Bank, 2000), 248; The World Bank, *World Development Indicators 1999* (Washington, D.C.: The World Bank, 1999), 254; The World Bank, *World Development Indicators 1998* (Washington, D.C.: The World Bank, 1998), 238; The World Bank, *World Development Indicators 1997* (Washington, D.C.: The World Bank, 1997), 219–220.

4. All the Caucasian and CA countries have suffered from growing debt, as reflected in Tables 3.9 and 3.10. This is a clear indicator of their worsening economic situation since independence, when they had no foreign debt at all (the Russian government exempted them from paying a share of the Soviet foreign debt). There is a simple reason for their growing debt: their limited agricultural and industrial exports do not generate enough funds to cover their imports. If the current economic situation persists, their increasing demand for imported agricultural and industrial products, which is a natural phenomenon given their growing populations, will worsen their debt burden.

TABLE 3.10   Growth in Burden of Debt in the Central Asian Countries (U.S.$ millions)

Year	Kazakhstan	Kyrgyzstan	Tajikistan	Turkmenistan	Uzbekistan
1998	5,714	1,148	1,070	2,266	3,162
1997	4,278	928	901	1,771	2,760
1996	2,920	789	707	825	2,319

Source: The World Bank, *World Development Indicators 2000* (Washington, D.C.: The World Bank, 2000), 249–250; The World Bank, *World Development Indicators 1999* (Washington, D.C.: The World Bank, 1999), 255–256; The World Bank, *World Development Indicators 1998* (Washington, D.C.: The World Bank, 1998), 239–240; The World Bank, *World Development Indicators 1997* (Washington, D.C.: The World Bank, 1997), 219–220.

The debt problem has become a major constraint to the economic development of the Caucasian and CA countries and has contributed to the prolongation of their transitional period. The repayment of debts and the associated service charges have consumed a significant portion of their annual revenues at a time when their limited financial resources have been inadequate to meet their growing needs. The heavy burden of debts has been quite evident from the magnitude of the respective service charges, which have taken a large percentage of the annual value of their exports. In 1997, this percentage was 5.8% for Armenia, 6.8% for Azerbaijan, 6.4% for Georgia, 6.5% for Kazakhstan, 6.3% for Kyrgyzstan, 4.6% for Tajikistan, 34.7% for Turkmenistan, and 12.9% for Uzbekistan.[14] In 1998, in Azerbaijan the percentage of debt service to exports decreased to 2.3%; however, this percentage increased in all other cases: 8.9% for Armenia, 7.6% for Georgia, 13% for Kazakhstan, 9.4% for Kyrgyzstan, 13.7% for Tajikistan, 42% for Turkmenistan, and 13.2% Uzbekistan.[15]

5. All the Caucasian and CA countries have suffered from high inflation rates for most of their independence era. As indicated in Tables 3.11 and 3.12, they all experienced three-digit inflation rates in the 1990s. Of course, there have been differences in terms of these rates among those countries, and therefore the negative impact of inflation on their economies has varied from country to country. However, there is no doubt that high inflation has contributed to the exhaustion of their weak economies. This phenomenon was especially devastating in the first few years of independence, when four-digit rates (such as 2,140% in Tajikistan) was a norm all over the Caucasus and Central Asia.[16] The inflation rate has dropped to one- or two-digit figures since 1998. As a result, its negative impact has reduced significantly, although the Caucasian and CA countries still suffer from inflation to a varying extent. For example, in ascending order, in 1998 the inflation rate was –8.3% in Azerbaijan, 3.4% in Georgia, 4.9% in Kazakhstan, 11.2% in Armenia, 11.5% in Kyrgyzstan, 13.5% in Turkmenistan, 33.2% in Uzbekistan, and 49.9% in Tajikistan.[17] Nevertheless, these lower rates compared to those of the early 1990s are deceptive because the weak and declining economies of all these countries are susceptible to sharp fluctuations in inflation rates. Such rates could easily go up if their current dismal economic performance continues.

TABLE 3.11   Average Percentage Rate of Inflation in the Caucasus, 1990–98

Armenia	Azerbaijan	Georgia
349.1	322.3	709.3

Source: UNDP, *Human Development Report 2000* (New York: Oxford University Press, 2000), 203.

6. Finally, to different extents, all Caucasian and CA countries suffer from a shortage of trained human resources. The lack of sufficient scientists, engineers, managers, technicians, and skilled workers has created a major economic hindrance, which contributes to the prolongation of their transitional period. The root cause of this problem can be traced back to the Soviet era. At that time, most of the highly trained or highly educated members of the workforce in these countries were Slavs and mainly Russians.[18] In the postindependence period, many of them have left for Russia or immigrated to Western countries and Israel, for reasons ranging from discrimination to unemployment.[19] Hence, there is a severe shortage of educated and trained personnel in all the eight Caucasian and CA countries. In particular, there is an acute shortage of managers at a time when their privatized state enterprises and the state enterprises themselves require large numbers of trained and experienced managers to expand and improve their operations. The overwhelming majority of those who have remained in these countries, whether Russian, Caucasian, or Central Asian, were trained in the Soviet era to run a highly centralized command economy. They are therefore not fully qualified to deal with

TABLE 3.12   Average Percentage Rate of Inflation in Central Asia, 1990–98

Kazakhstan	Kyrgyzstan	Tajikistan	Turkmenistan	Uzbekistan
330.7	157.8	300	663.4	356.7

Source: UNDP, *Human Development Report 2000* (New York: Oxford University Press, 2000), 203–204.

the economic difficulties of the transitional period, which require knowledge about and experience in free-enterprise economies. Managerial problems therefore contribute to the poor performance of the Caucasian and CA economies.

In short, the economic situation in the Caucasian and CA countries has not only not improved since independence, but has worsened significantly. Their deteriorating economies have made the Caucasians and the Central Asians hesitant about the implementation of economic reforms to complete the transitional period. They have all embarked on some degree of reform, including launching national currencies, liberalizing prices, overhauling their tax systems, and introducing phased privatization.[20] The extent of these reforms does, of course, differ from country to country. However, despite differences in the extent of their reform programs, the Caucasian and CA governments have all slowed down the pace of their economic reform. This lowering of pace has been especially visible in the areas of the privatization of industrial and agricultural enterprises and the removal of subsidies. Fear of their predictable outcome has been the main reason for this change of plan. In the absence of a growing economy capable of generating adequate employment opportunities and sensible incomes, an extensive and fast-paced economic reform will inevitably lead to massive unemployment and poverty.

In particular, these economic ills will be the inevitable result of massive privatization in the Caucasian and CA countries, whose states owned almost the entire economic units in the rural and urban areas at the time of independence. In the Soviet era, many factors led to overstaffing of government departments and of farming and industrial enterprises. The most important factors were poor management, use of old machinery or production techniques, and the absence of profit-making as the main economic objective. A major privatization of these entities will justify the extensive downsizing of personnel and therefore massive unemployment, which is necessary to make them profitable. Even the half-hearted economic reforms of the postindependence era have worsened the unemployment situation drastically. A good example is Georgia: despite positive growth rates over the last few years, in early 2001 it suffered from massive unemployment. Although the official registered number of unemployed people was only 100,000, 25% of its total workforce of three million (i.e., 750,000) was estimated to be unemployed.[21] Thanks to statistical juggling, they were not considered officially as unemployed as they were on indefinite, forced, unpaid leave.[22] Apart from the fear of unemployment, the Caucasians and the Central Asians cannot possibly cope with the combined effects of rising prices and lowering income without the existing government subsidies, at least for their most essential daily needs such as foodstuffs. It is no wonder that their governments have lost their enthusiasm for large-scale economic reforms and have postponed them to a time when their economies are in a better shape. Given the worsening economic situation, the resumption of such reform may not begin in the foreseeable future.

POLITICAL SITUATION

The collapse of the Soviet Union in 1991 weakened practically all Caucasian and CA institutions inherited from the Soviet era. The only exception initially was the political system, which seemed unchallenged and stable. Unlike most other former Soviet republics such as the Baltic republics and the Ukraine, the independence of the Caucasian and CA republics was not the result of long and widespread mass movements and antigovernment activities demanding fundamental changes. For that matter, their political system survived independence and remained almost intact, giving their leaders the ability to run their countries with a more or less functional state apparatus. In all these countries except Kyrgyzstan, the ex-Communist party chiefs monopolizing political power in the Soviet era became the leaders of the newly independent states. In the postindependence era, the Soviet political, economic, and military elite dominated practically all aspects of life in all these countries including Kyrgyzstan. The political systems of the eight Caucasian and CA countries have faced challenges threatening their stability and very existence during this era. The extent and impact of such challenges varies from region to region and from country to country. A brief analysis of the political situation in the two regions should shed light on this argument.

The three Caucasian countries—Azerbaijan, Armenia, and Georgia—have all experienced severe political and military challenges, shaking the very roots of their states. Internal and external destabilizing forces in various forms have challenged the authority and the legitimacy of their political systems. Over thirteen years after its appearance in a bloody form, Azerbaijan and Armenia have yet to settle their territorial dispute over Nagorno Karabakh, an Armenian-dominated enclave in Azerbaijan.[23] Armenia had territorial claim to the enclave in the Soviet era, but it only became an active claim in 1988 when its Armenian inhabitants expressed their aspiration for unification with Armenia. This quickly escalated to a bloody war between Azerbaijan and Armenia, along with its militant protégé groups in Nagorno Karabakh. The war outlived the Soviet Union and continued until 1994. The two sides then agreed on a ceasefire, which left 20% of Azeri land, including the disputed territory, under Armenian control. Being considered by all states as part of Azerbaijan, the unsettled dispute over Nagorno Karabakh and the continued occupation of another part of Azerbaijan—the Lachin Passage, which connects the disputed enclave to Armenia—have created a strong sentiment of hostility between the two neighboring countries. Efforts toward the settlement of this conflict have all failed. The political, economic, security, and emotional significance of the issue for both sides has made them uninterested in a compromise, which seems to be the only solution for a peaceful settlement of the dispute. As the humiliated party to the conflict, Azerbaijan has seen no room for a compromise. It lost 20% of its territory during about six years of bloody and devastating war with Armenia. As a result, over one million Azeris—about 15% of its population—have been forced to leave their homes, which are now under Armenian control. They have since moved to other parts of Azerbaijan, living as refugees in poor conditions. Not surprisingly, they have formed a major force opposing any settlement of the Azeri–Armenian conflict, which leaves parts of their land under Armenian authority. Heavy casualties and destruction inflicted by the Armenians on the Azeris have made the rest of the population supportive of this uncompromising attitude. In such a situation, the Azeri government—blamed by its people for the humiliating defeat at the hands of its smaller and less populous neighbor—has found no justification for a compromise with the Armenians. Given the circumstances, such a compromise would inevitably delegitimize its authority and contribute to a sudden eruption of dissent by its population at large. Given a prevailing general dissatisfaction with the overall situation, this is a type of risk that the Azeri government cannot afford to take.

On their part, the Armenians have not been any more eager to compromise. The unification of the Armenian-dominated Nagorno Karabakh with Armenia has been a very emotional issue around which the Armenians have been united since 1988.[24] Over time, this issue has become a defining characteristic of Armenian nationalism. It is no wonder that all the Armenian nationalist groups oppose any compromise with Azerbaijan, demanding the return or partial return of Nagorno Karabakh. On the contrary, they advocate the unification of that territory and other occupied Azeri territories with Armenia. Added to this, three major factors have ruled out a compromise on the part of the Armenians. One has been the need of small Armenia for more land and population to make its republic a viable political entity. This practical and security-related factor has been a major obstacle to efforts for convincing Armenia to return the occupied Azeri territories to Azerbaijan. Another factor has been the fact that the Karabkahis— the Armenian residents of Nagorno Karabakh—have declared independence from Azerbaijan and run their territory as an independent country. In the absence of a regional or international supportive mood for their unification with Armenia, the Armenians and the Kharabakhis have considered independence as the best temporary option, despite their will for an immediate unification. In such a situation, the prevailing nationalist mood in the territory simply writes off its return to Azerbaijan as an option. Insistence on such a scenario would only lead to an intra-ethnic conflict unacceptable for the Armenians. Finally, the strength of the so-called Karabakhis within the Armenian political system and society has practically made a compromise by the Armenians out of the question. The Karabakhis, who are the staunch supporters of the unification of their land with Armenia, have become fully integrated in Armenian society and its political apparatus. They have achieved high offices in the government and in the military, which has given them the practical power to influence Armenian policies toward Azerbaijan and the disputed territory. Suffice it to state here that the current president of Armenia, Robert Kocharian, is a Karabakhi. In short, the Armenians have their own reasons for not being enthusiastic for a compromise.

Given the importance of the occupied Azeri territories for both parties to the conflict, all the mediatory efforts by different regional and nonregional countries or groups of countries have failed so far. They include those of the OECD (Organization for Economic Cooperation and Development) and the OSCE (Organization for Security and Cooperation in Europe) aimed at making the two sides negotiate for a peaceful settlement of the dispute. The failure of a decade of such efforts has suggested that the two sides are too far apart on this issue to settle their conflict through negotiation. The most recent example substantiating this statement was the refusal of Azeri President Haidar Aliev and Armenian President Robert Kocharian to attend a pre-agreed summit meeting in Geneva in June 2001. In May 2001, Armenian Foreign Ministry spokeswoman Dziunik Aghadjanian announced the indefinite postponement of the meeting.[25] Both sides have reportedly stated as the main reason for the postponement their respective peoples' lack of preparedness for a compromise. In the absence of a realistic possibility for a mutually acceptable solution to the Azeri–Armenian dispute, the continuation of the current no-war–no-peace state of relations between Armenia and Azerbaijan has created a situation prone to a sudden resumption of war.

Besides the Armenian–Azeri territorial dispute, there have been other sources of political challenges in both Armenia and Azerbaijan. Various factors have contributed to their internal strife and political uncertainty. Internal conflicts have negatively affected Armenian–Azeri relations, because the ongoing territorial dispute and the search for its resolution have become major sources of political rivalry and political tension in both countries. The two countries have experienced a volatile political environment since independence. Rivalry between and among various political factions forming their respective political ruling elite has marked their history since independence. Armenia has experienced years of intra-elite conflicts under both the current president, Robert Kocharian, and his predecessor, Levond Ter-Petrosian. Its postindependence history has been characterized by numerous arrests, trials, imprisonments, and assassinations of senior politicians charged with corruption, murder, and conspiracy against the government. The government, some of its factions, or some of its forming figures have been implicated in murders or murder attempts of politicians, including active senior ones. The most recent blatant example was the massacre, by a rival group, of Prime Minister Vazgen Sarkissian and the speaker of parliament along with six members of parliament in October 1999.[26]

The situation has been especially turbulent in Azerbaijan. The 1992 election of Abulfazel Elchibey as president initiated a short period of rule by pan-Turkists in that country.[27] His administration was characterized by consecutive defeats in its war with Armenia and by rampant corruption. President Elchibey rapidly lost his legitimacy and initial attractiveness, as his tough remarks about Armenia fascinated many Azeris who had been humiliated by the Armenians on the battleground. Upon his fall in 1993, Haidar Aliev, the ex-Communist party boss of Azerbaijan, took power. Like his predecessor, he was unable to reverse the military defeat of the Azeris and had to accept a ceasefire in 1994, which left about 20% of Azerbaijan's land under Armenian control. He still continues to rule over Azerbaijan. The Aliev era has been marked with instability and the growing weakness of the Azeri state.[28] Several abortive coups and subsequent purges of the military and civilian elite suspected of masterminding them have seriously damaged its legitimacy and credibility. In addition, they have narrowed support for the state among the Azeri elite. The Aliev administration's inability to recapture its country's occupied territories, the worsening economic situation with a direct impact on the average Azeris, the suppression of all types of antigovernment activities, and the growing authoritarianism have sharply reduced its popularity. Added to these, the rampant corruption within the government, the civil service, and the ruling elite has damaged its legitimacy. In particular, the Aliev family's monopolization of practically all major political institutions and economic facilities has created a very strong sense of resentment among the Azeris, who are struggling to meet their ends. As an example, President Aliev's son, Ilham Aliev, is the president of the State Oil Company of Azerbaijan (SOCAR), while many of his relatives and friends dominate the 125-member parliament of Azerbaijan, including his son-in-law and brother.

If the political situation has been bad in Armenia and Azerbaijan, it has been even worse in Georgia. The Georgian state has been weakened by a variety of severe political and military challenges to its authority. Two major secessionist movements in Abkhazia and South Ossetia, in which Russia has significant influence, have seriously damaged the sovereignty of the Georgian state and undermined its territorial integrity.[29] The former has also sought reunification with Russia. The two movements engaged in a military confrontation with the Georgian forces until late 1992 (South Ossetia) and 1993 (Abkazia) when the civil war ended with the defeat of the Georgian forces and the effective independence of those regions. Efforts to find a peaceful solution to the problem have all failed so far. The failure has created a fragile situation that is conducive to the resumption of civil war at any moment. The current uncertain situation cannot continue indefinitely. For the Georgian government, its practical loss of control over about half of its territory is totally unacceptable. For the secessionists, the situation is no more acceptable. Facing a severe economic decline, they cannot embark on any major economic plan because of their uncertain situation. This predicament has denied them both the economic assistance of the Georgian government and that of potential foreign donors.

In addition to the secessionist movements, Georgia has also suffered from an internal military and political conflict since 1992. In that year, the ousting from power of President Zviad Gamsakhurdia initiated a civil war that has lasted on and off ever since. Despite his "suicide" or "murder" in 1993, his followers have challenged the authority of the Georgian government through military operations of different magnitude. Their continuous low-level military operations have occasionally grown into major ones, such as their late-1999 intrusion into Tbilisi, Georgia's capital.[30] They have also resorted to various types of political actions, which have usually turned violent. As a recent example, in May 2001 about 600 supporters of the deceased president clashed with the Georgian police.[31] The event escalated to violence as the supporters unsuccessfully tried to stage an unsanctioned demonstration in Tbilisi to mark the tenth anniversary of Gamsakhurdia's election as president. At least 25 police officers were reported as injured, and an unspecified number of the demonstrators were arrested.[32]

There are also other forces or factors challenging or weakening the state of Georgia. These include different warlords who have weakened the authority of the Georgian government since independence. The latter controlled various parts of the country until 1995 when, two years after his election, President Shevernadzhe established its authority in the areas outside the separatist territories. Apart from political challenges, the expanding criminal groups involved in all kinds of illegal activities, including international drug-trafficking, have seriously challenged internal security. They have operated almost freely in all parts of the country, including in Tbilisi. Yet they have certain strongholds such as in the autonomous republic of Ajaria, which is not under the control of the Georgian government. Aslan Abashidze, a warlord, runs the region as he wishes.[33] Finally, rampant corruption among the ruling elite has narrowed support for the central government among the population. Continuation of corruption, despite the government's annual pledges to uproot it, has damaged the government's legitimacy.[34] All these destabilizing and centrifugal forces have severely weakened the Georgian state. Several assassination attempts on President Shevernadzhe, attributed both to the sessionists and also to the dissatisfied factions within the government, have symbolically demonstrated the state's political fragility.

In short, the three Caucasian states have tolerated many challenges of different natures to their authority. The major challenges have continued to this date and are likely to continue in the foreseeable future. Added to these, the economic deterioration of the three Caucasian countries, the falling living standards, and the rampant corruption have all contributed to a growing dissatisfaction among their peoples. This widespread dissatisfaction has found its way into internal politics, in the form of growing tension within the ruling elite and the rise of political opposition. All these factors have severely damaged the authority and legitimacy of the three Caucasian states and have contributed to their long-term instability.

In comparison to the Caucasus, Central Asia has been more stable since independence. With the exception of Tajikistan, which has experienced a civil war, the CA states have not faced significant challenges to their authority and have enjoyed internal stability. Nevertheless, to different extents, there is the potential for instability in all the CA countries. In Tajikistan, a peace treaty in June 1997 ended five years of civil war.[35] After about four years of negotiations and cooperation, the two sides to the conflict—the Muslim-Democratic coalition and the Tajik government—have not yet achieved the goals set in the peace treaty; many issues are still to be addressed. The civil war is over, but the country still suffers from political instability and uncertainty. This is partly due to certain political factors. The destructive efforts of anti-peace-treaty forces on both sides of the Tajik conflict and the alleged intervention of Uzbekistan in the internal affairs of Tajikistan are two main factors. The Uzbek government reportedly masterminded the abortive 1999 coup in Tajikistan, staged by mainly ethnic Uzbeks of Tajikistan.[36] Persistence of economic problems is also partly responsible for the current unstable situation. The main social and economic causes of the civil war—for example, severe regional disparities, underdevelopment, and clan politics—are still well in place. Unless the Tajiks receive a substantial amount of foreign assistance, their worsening economy and the underdevelopment of the country will likely reignite the civil conflict.

The other CA countries have not experienced instability in the form of civil war, but they have become increasingly concerned about instability in their region and in their own countries. On the one hand, the Taliban-ruled Afghanistan was, until the removal of the Taliban from the political scene in November 2001, a direct threat to the security of three neighboring CA states, Turkmenistan, Uzbekistan, and Tajikistan.[37] Afghanistan is the ethnic mirror of Central Asia. For that matter, the spillover of the Afghan civil war into these CA countries has been a feasible scenario since their independence in 1991, which will likely destabilize the entire region. This threat has remained in place despite the formation of the interim government in Afghanistan and the cessation of the war between the Northern Alliance forces and the Taliban. The situation is still ripe for another round of civil war between and among different Afghan groups representing different ethnic groups, who could be dissatisfied with their share of power in the central government. In January 2002, the outbreak of bloody fighting between Pashtun groups over the control of certain Pashtun areas, despite the appointment of a governor for them by the interim government, clearly reflected the possibility of the resumption of civil war.

On the other hand, poor economic performance and increasing social and economic problems are contributing to the rise of mass political dissent. Uzbekistan, which is known as the most stable country in Central Asia, has been experiencing political challenges with a long-term negative impact on its stability. It has been facing the rise of mass opposition in its Andijan Province, located in the troublesome Ferghana Valley. As discussed in Chapters 4 and 5, the growing instability in the valley has the potential to destabilize the three countries sharing it—namely, Kyrgyzstan, Tajikistan, and Uzbekistan—while creating grounds for instability in other CA countries. Uzbekistan has also suffered from violent antigovernment activities elsewhere. The recent incidents include the explosion of a series of bombs in early 1999 in its capital, Tashkent, which demonstrated the vulnerability of the Uzbek state.[38]

The government of Kyrgyzstan has not faced major and extensive challenges for most of its postindependence era. However, certain factors have sharply damaged its legitimacy. The most important of these are, on the one hand, the gradual monopolization of political and economic power within the hands of President Askar Akaev (Agaev) and his closed circle of allies and, on the other, the expanding corruption within the ruling elite, the government, and the civil service. The growing authoritarianism in what was once the most democratic CA country and the increasing restrictions on the activities of political parties and on individual freedoms and rights have paved the way for future eruption of popular dissatisfaction. The rising instability in the form of armed conflict in Kyrgyzstan's part of the Ferghana Valley such as in Bateken (Beteken) could pose a serious challenge to the Kyrgyz state. The following chapters elaborate on this possibility.

The other two CA countries, Kazakhstan and Turkmenistan, have so far avoided any significant security threat targeting their respective states. In addition to growing authoritarianism, other factors have helped the government of Kazakhstan prevent major security challenges to its power. The peculiar ethnic makeup of the country has been a major contributing factor. The weak numerical strength of the ethnic Kazakh, who constituted about 40% of the population at the time of independence and about 50% a decade after, has inclined them to rally behind their government despite its several weaknesses, including corruption. The large Russian ethnic minority, forming about 40% of the population, has also had its own reason for not challenging the administration of President Nursultan Nazarbaev. The peculiar ethnic structure of Kazakhstan has motivated the president to observe the rights of the minorities to a large extent and to seek their integration into the country, in recognition of his country's need for friendly ties with its neighboring Russia for economic and political reasons. It is also a clear sign of his concern about the threat of Russia's direct intervention in his country's internal affairs. Being a neighbor, Russia has the opportunity and the means to intervene, as Kazakhstan's large Russian ethnic community provides a social basis and an excuse for such an action. Moreover, the need of his country for the ethnic Russians, which account for most of the educated and skilled population as a consequence of the Soviet preferential policy, has created another incentive for President Nazarbaev to appease them. His accommodating approach has inclined the ethnic Russians—who are not welcome in Russia, a neighboring country struggling with its many major economic challenges—to support his government, by and large.

Given the circumstances, the Nazarbaev administration has seemed to be the best available option for the time being, despite its shortcomings. Balancing Kazakh nationalism with the recognition of minority rights has helped the Kazakh government prevent the eruption of major antigovernment movements. Yet many factors will likely contribute to the emergence of ethnic dissent in different forms with major implications for the Kazakh state. These include Kazakhstan's worsening economy, growing Kazakh nationalism, and the increasing interest of Russia in reestablishing itself in the ex-Soviet republics.

In Turkmenistan, the high-handed policy of President Safarmorad Niyazov (Turkmenbashi) has left no room for any type of dissent. His autocratic political system, characterized by his cult of personality, has so far prevented the emergence of challenging forces to the Turkmen state. Despite its strong appearance, this personified state deriving legitimacy from its leader cannot be a guarantee against instability. The disappearance of the president from the political scene for one reason or another, including death, will likely lead to the sudden collapse of the Turkmen state. In such a case, the eruption of the long-suppressed dissent will be a very probable scenario.

In short, if the current situation continues, the sheer exercise of suppression (e.g., in Turkmenistan and Uzbekistan) and balancing acts (in Kazakhstan) will hardly be enough to prevent the eruption of opposition. Unless the basic needs of the people are guaranteed and meaningful and sustainable steps made toward an overhaul of the ailing economies, all CA states will likely be drawn into instability in one form or another in the near future.

SOCIAL SITUATION

The collapse of the Soviet Union and independence had a major impact on the social structure of the eight Caucasian and CA countries. The Soviet collapse and the ensuing economic paralysis provoked fundamental changes in social institutions. The collapse ended the ideological legitimacy of the political apparatus and its ruling elite and discredited the command-economy system and its social norms and institutions. The disappearance of the unifying ideology advocating equality among Soviet citizens regardless of their social background and personal attributes, on the one hand, and the sudden lowering of living standards, on the other, opened the door to the rise of long-suppressed sentiments and discriminatory social attitudes. Hence, nationalism, localism, regionalism, tribalism, clan politics, and gender discrimination reemerged in the post-Soviet era. With the exception of

tribalism, which is peculiar to the countries with a strong tribal structure—namely, Kazakhstan, Kyrgyzstan, and Turkmenistan—all these
other social phenomena have existed in the entire Caucasian and CA
countries, but, of course, to differing extents. This situation has formed
a recipe for violence against minorities and discrimination in all aspects of life, based on one's sex and/or affiliation with a region, tribe,
clan, or ethnic group.

Certain social strata and low-income social groups have been the
major victims of this negative social trend, although almost all the
Caucasians and Central Asians have suffered in the postindependence
era in one way or another. Women, children and youth, pensioners,
civil servants, academics, and scientists—who together constitute the
overwhelming majority of the Caucasian and CA populations—have
experienced a steady loss in their social status. Many preindependence
guaranteed rights and privileges for these social groups no longer
exist, while others are being eroded. The eroding social safety net and
the declining educational system reduce their chances and hopes for an
acceptable future. Women increasingly face discrimination in social,
economic, educational, and political fields, aimed at reducing their
role outside the home.[39] In particular, women face discrimination in
the area of employment. They are in effect encouraged to leave the
work force as they are losing the Soviet privileges that enabled them to
work outside home while raising their children. Prolonged maternity
leave is an example. In Turkmenistan, for example, women may
receive up to four years' maternity leave, but without salary.[40] An
increasing number of women are laid off from jobs or excluded from
certain positions.[41] Unemployment rates are much higher for women.[42]
Of course, there are differences among the eight Caucasian and CA
countries in terms of the impact of the postindependence era on the
participation of women in the workforce, but their declining percentage of the workforce has been a trend in all of them, with the exception
of Armenia. Two examples, each pertaining to one of the two regions,
should demonstrate this trend. In Georgia and Tajikistan, the percentage of women from the workforce dropped from 49.3% in 1980 to
46.6% in 1998, and from 46.9% in 1980 to 44.3% in 1998, respectively.[43] In Armenia, their percentage jumped from 47.9% in 1980 to
48.4% in 1998.[44] Far from an orchestrated effort of the Armenian
government, this is most probably a result of the fatal impact of the
Azeri–Armenian war on Armenia's male population and the higher

rate of emigration among the Armenian men. Apart from the employment situation, in health the level of services is decreasing for women. Shorter life expectancy and rising cases of anemia are just two indicators of lowering health standards.[45] In particular, health services for pregnant women are eroding, a clear retreat from the extensive services available preindependence.[46] In education, enrollment rates are no longer universal. The number of school dropouts is larger among girls than among boys.[47]

Children and youth are also victims of rapid social and economic changes. Education is no longer free for all Caucasian and CA nationals. State-subsidized kindergartens are being closed, and the pattern of preference for boys in schooling is emerging among families.[48] As elsewhere in the former Soviet republics, prostitution and crime are expanding all over the region.[49] With social services continuing to decline, children and youth are becoming more vulnerable. They suffer from the crumbling educational and health systems as well as from nutritional problems. The elderly or pensioners have lost their Soviet-granted guarantee of an adequate standard of living.

Forming the overwhelming majority of the Caucasians and Central Asians, low-income urban and rural social groups have had a hard time meeting their basic needs since independence. Like other Caucasians and Central Asians, they suffer from loss of employment, lowering income and purchasing power, and rising prices. The effect of this worsening economic situation on the Caucasians and Central Asians has been devastating, as independence suddenly lowered their living standards sharply, a process that has continued to this date. In the absence of a significant private sector offering alternative economic opportunities and better-paid employment, it has been extremely difficult for the majority of people to cope. Excluding an insignificant percentage of self-employed people, the rest of the population have been civil servants working for their government in the rural or urban areas on preindependence salaries. These salaries were small in absolute terms. Living in a highly subsidized socialist country, where all prices were artificially set to ensure a minimum living standard for all its citizens, did not require large salaries or significant personal savings. The purchasing power of the Caucasian and Central Asians has drastically decreased, a phenomenon caused by their small salaries, which have increased only slightly (in real terms) from their preindependence levels, and also by their lack of savings. As a result, coping with the new situation has become very difficult for the average person.

The removal or reduction of subsidies, the total cut or decrease in many essential social services (e.g., health, food, education, and transportation), and the erosion of the social safety net have had serious social implications. While almost everyone suffers from the loss or reduction of these services, economically vulnerable social groups, who were well protected before the fall of the USSR, suffer more. These include low-income social groups, pensioners, certain groups of women (working, pregnant, lactating, and single mothers), and children. The removal or reduction of necessary services and subsidies especially affects those who had long been the beneficiaries of such egalitarian measures in the Soviet era. The decreasing purchasing power of average nationals of the Caucasus and Central Asia and the rising prices have pushed many of them into poverty. Poverty is widespread and extremely high. In Georgia, for example, about 90% of the population was estimated to live below the poverty line in 2000.[50] The situation is more or less the same elsewhere. The high crime rate, especially among the youth, is a clear indicator of the expansion of poverty and lack of opportunities for a decent, normal life.

In addition, ethnic minorities have experienced difficulties whose extent varies from country to country. The rising nationalism in all the newly independent Caucasian and CA countries has removed the social protection for ethnic minorities. Hostility toward ethnic minorities has translated itself into discrimination against minorities in education, employment, and social life. To a varying extent, all ethnic minorities experience a form of discrimination. However, the largest target group has been the Slavic minority groups of the Caucasian and CA countries—in particular, the Russians. The latter have been mainly considered as the remnants of the former colonial power, Russia. To a far lesser extent, anti-Semitism has also emerged in those countries. The anti-Russian sentiment was very strong in the first few years of independence, but it has subsided to a significant extent. Among other factors, this phenomenon has forced many Slavs and, in particular, Russians to leave for Russia or Western countries. During the period 1989–98, the number of Russians decreased all over the Caucasus and Central Asia. This has not been very significant in the former, which have very small Russian communities. In the latter, the situation has been very different as it hosts large Russian communities. The percentage of Russian people from the total population of each CA country has dropped sharply in the two countries with the largest Russian communities—that is, in Kazakhstan, from 37% to 31%, and in Kyrgyzstan, from 21% to 14.6%.[51] The decreased percentage has also been significant in other CA countries—that is, in Tajikistan, from 7.6% to 6%, in Turkmenistan, from 9.5% to 7%, and in Uzbekistan, from 8.3% to 6.5%.[52] The worsening economic situation, rising unemployment, and shortages of many necessities such as housing have created barriers to mass migration to Russia of many ethnic Russians of Central Asia. Even at its current level, the migration of Russians has intensified the economic and social problems of the transitional period. While having a negative impact on both regions, this has been especially true for Central Asia. The latter's ethnic Russians dominated most of the regional political, economic, military, scientific, medical, and higher-education institutions until 1991.[53] The resulting brain drain has reduced local capabilities for restructuring the CA countries, with possible prolonged effects on the transitional period. This situation has further damaged their economies, as they are now suffering from a shortage of qualified employees.

NOTES

1. UNDP, *World Development Report 2000* (New York: UNDP, 2000), 215.

2. The World Bank, *World Development Indicators 2000* (Washington, D.C.: The World Bank, 2000), 38–40.

3. Michael Lelyveld, *Azerbaijan: Caspian Region Faces Fuel Shortages*, Radio Free Europe/Radio Liberty (REF/RL), 3 February 2000, 1 (internet text).

4. Ibid., 1, 2.

5. "Uzbekistan," *Eurasian File* (Ankara), 133 (August 2000), 5; "Increasing the Quality of Kyrgyz Tobacco," *Eurasian File* (Ankara), 138 (January 2001), 12.

6. The World Bank, *World Development Indicators—2000* (Washington, D.C.: The World Bank, 2000), 182.

7. Kyrgyz Republic/Tajikistan: Country Report—4th quarter 1998, 33–34.

8. Economist Intelligence Unit, *Kazakhstan: Country Profile 1998–99* (London: Economist Intelligence Unit, 1998), 47.

9. Ibid., 48.

10. UNDP, *Human Development Report 2000* (New York: Oxford University Press, 2000), 211.

11. Ibid., 211.

12. "Economic Indicators in Azerbaijan," *Eurasian File* (Ankara), 139 (February 2001), 2

13. UNDP, *Human Development Report 2000*, 211–212.

14. UNDP, *Human Development Report 1999* (New York: Oxford University Press, 1999), 194.

15. *Human Development Report 2000*, 220.

16. Jeni Klugman and George Schrieber, "Survey of Health Reform in Central Asia," in *Implementing Health Sector Reform in Central Asia: Paper from a Health Policy Seminar Held in Ashgabat, Turkmenistan, June 1996*, ed. Zuzana Feachem, Martin Hensher, and Laura Rose (Washington, D.C.: The World Bank, 1999), 22.

17. UNDP, *Human Development Report 2000*, 203–204.

18. Martin Klatt, "Russians in the 'Near abroad,'" *REF/RL Research Report, 3*, No. 32 (19 August 1994), 40.

19. Judith T. Shuval and Judith H. Bernstein, eds., *Immigrant Physicians: Former Soviet Doctors in Israel, Canada, and the United States* (Westport, CT: Praeger, 1997).

20. Shirin Akiner, "Social and Political Reorganization in Central Asia: Transition from Pre-Colonial to Post-Colonial Society," in *Post-Soviet Central Asia* (London: Tauris Academic Studies, 1998), 22.

21. Jean-Christophe Peuch, "Georgia: Corruption Seen as the Norm," REF/RL, 10 May 2001.

22. Ibid.

23. For an account on the roots of the Armenian-Azeri conflict over Nagorno Karabakh, see Alieh Arfaei, "Nagorno Karabakh's Sad Case," *Majelieh-e Motaellat-e Asyaie Markazi va Ghafghaz [Central Asia and the Caucasus Review]* (Tehran), 1, No. 2 (Autumn 1992), 153–206.

24. For an analysis of the significance of Nagorno Karabakh for the Armenians, see Herand Passdarmachian, *History of Armenia* (Tehran: Zarrin Publishers, 1999); see also Naser Takmil Homayun, "A Glance at Karabakh in Iran's History," *Majelieh-e Motaellat-e Asyaie Markazi va Ghafghaz [Central Asia and the Caucasus Review]* (Tehran), 2, No. 1 (Summer 1993), 59–98.

25. REF/RL web journal, "Transcaucasia and Central Asia," 29 May 2001.

26. Bahram Amirahmadian, "The Trend of Developments in the Karabakh Crisis," *Majelieh-e Motaellat-e Asyaie Markazi va Ghafghaz [Central Asia and the Caucasus Review]* (Tehran), 28 (Winter 2000), 30.

27. For an account on the Elichibey era, see Hooman Peimani, *Iran and the*

United States: The Rise of the West Asian Regional Grouping (Westport, CT: Praeger, 1999), 35–36.

28. For details about the Aliev era, see Hooman Peimani, *The Caspian Pipeline Dilemma: Political Games and Economic Losses* (Westport, CT: Praeger, 2001), 82–84.

29. For an account on the secessionist movements in Georgia, see Valery Shaldiz, "The Ossetian Crisis in Georgia," *Majelieh-e Motaellat-e Asyaie Markazi va Ghafghaz* [*Central Asia and the Caucasus Review*] (Tehran), 2, No. 1 (Summer 1993), 161–168; see also Hojatolah Faghani, "The Eastward Expansion of NATO: A Review of the Georgia's Position," *Majelieh-e Motaellat-e Asyaie Markazi va Ghafghaz* [*Central Asia and the Caucasus Review*] (Tehran), No. 26 (Summer 1999),19–30.

30. Peimani, *Caspian Pipeline Dilemma*, 88.

31. REF/RL web journal, "Transcaucasia and Central Asia," 29 May 2001.

32. Ibid.

33. Jean-Christophe Peuch, "Caucasus: Georgia Sees Future in Regional Cooperation," REF/RL web journal, 11 May 2001.

34. Jean-Christophe Peuch, "Georgia: Corruption Seen As the 'Norm,'" REF/RL web journal, 10 May 2001.

35. For an account on the factors contributing to the Tajik civil war and also on the peace process, see: Hooman Peimani, *Regional Security and the Future of Central Asia: The Competition of Iran, Turkey, and Russia* (Westport, CT: Praeger, 1998), 28–30, 32–33, 66–67.

36. Dilip Hiro, Failed Revolt, *Middle East International* (25 December 1998), 19.

37. For an analysis on the destabilizing impact of the Taliban on the neighboring countries of Afghanistan, see Ziba Farzin-nia, "The Emergence of the Taliban on the Afghan Scene," *Majelieh-e Motaellat-e Asyaie Markazi va Ghafghaz* [*Central Asia and the Caucasus Review*] (Tehran), 23 (Fall 1998), 15–28.

38. Dilip Hiro, "Bomb Blasts in Tashkent," *Middle East International* (12 March 1999), 16.

39. Jeanne Koopman, *Gender Issues in Farm Restructuring in Uzbekistan and Kyrgyzstan: Implications for the BASIS Research Program* (Washington, D.C.: International Research on Women and BASIS Project, Land Tenure Center, April 1998); *To Beijing and Beyond: The Gender Gap in Eastern Europe and the Commonwealth of Independent States (CIS) and the Baltic States- NGO Forum, Beijing* (New York: UNDP, 1995).

40. *Women and Gender in Countries in Transition: A UNICEF Perspective* (New York: UNICEF, 1995).

41. Ibid.

42. Ibid.

43. UNDP, *World Development Indicators 2000*, 46, 48.

44. Ibid., 46.

45. See: UNDP annual publication, *Human Development Report*, for the period 1992–98; Almaz Sharmanov, "Anaemia in Central Asia: Demographic and Health Survey Experience," *Food and Nutrition Bulletin*, 19, No.4 (1998), 307–318.

46. Ibid.

47. Ibid.

48. Ibid.

49. Ibid.

50. Sozar Subelian, "Turning Over a New Leaf In Tbilisi?" Institute for War & Peace Reporting, Caucasus Reporting Service, 10 Jan 2000, 08:44:04 EST.

51. "Central Asia: The Shrinking Hordes," *The Economist,* 3 April 1999, 53.

52. Ibid.

53. Farhad Attaie, "A Retrospective Glance at the History and the Current Situation of the Central Asian Republics," *Majelieh-e Motaellat-e Asyaie Markazi va Ghafghaz* [*Central Asia and the Caucasus Review*] (Tehran), 1, No. 3 (Winter 1993), 158.

4

Rise of Authoritarianism

The fall of the USSR not only proved the bankruptcy of the Soviet leading ideology, it also demonstrated the illegitimacy of its despotic form of government. As in other Soviet regions, the rise of independent states in the Caucasus and Central Asia created the hope for a break in form and content with the past political system, which was characterized by despotic structures, values, and practices. The initial efforts of the Caucasian and CA leaders at dismantling the highly centralized Soviet command economy hinted at logical parallel efforts for uprooting its corresponding highly centralized political system, intolerant of any form of dissent. Hence there was an expectation among their peoples for the gradual creation of new political systems. The emerging new economic systems seemed to be encouraging their respective political systems to be based on democratic values and practices such as openness, transparency, and accountability. However, the reality has been a totally different story. Instead of a gradual democratization of their societies and political systems, all the Caucasian and CA ruling elites have (though not at the same point in time) opted for the formation of new undemocratic and dictatorial political systems. Without a doubt, their eight political systems are different in terms of extent of undemocratic nature and degree of toleration of dissent. There are also differences among them with respect to the form and speed of their formation. Regardless of such differences, in essence these political systems are all representative of an authoritarian type of government. The following analysis sheds light on the factors that have contributed to the emergence of authoritarianism in the Caucasus and Central Asia since independence. The influences contributing to its consolidation as the dominant model of governance in those regions are also discussed.

The period immediately after independence brought a degree of democracy to the newly independent states of the two regions. This was not at all the outcome of an envisaged plan for the democratization of those countries. Rather, it was the result of a sudden breakup of the Soviet system. In the final decade of the Soviet Union, the Gorbachev political reforms opened the highly closed Soviet political and social environment to some extent, but they did not lead to the democratization of the Soviet political and social systems.[1] In fact, those reforms mainly resulted in superficial changes in the Soviet Union as planned by the Soviet leadership. While granting a degree of personal freedom to the Soviet people, in practice they kept the totalitarian and the elitist nature of the political system intact. The fall of the Soviet Union in December 1991 suddenly opened the closed societies of its 15 republics and initiated a period of democratization. Far from reflecting the desire of their leaders, this was an unintentional and spontaneous process imposed by the circumstances on the Caucasian and CA ruling elites. The breakdown of the Soviet system and the unplanned and unexpected independence of its republics at a time when none of them was prepared to act as an independent state weakened the political apparatus at the republican level. The loss of the generous financial and nonfinancial assistance of the Soviet central government and the mass migration of most of the qualified people suddenly paralyzed republican political and economic life. This development left the Caucasian and CA governments without adequate means to run many of their government organizations, including those in charge of law enforcement and security. Hence, these governments were unable to maintain the tight grip they held on their respective countries during the Soviet era. Nor were their peoples prepared to accept the closed society of the Soviet era once all its economic, political, and ideological pillars were crumbling. The result was therefore the breakdown of the police state, which created an unintentional relatively free environment, to the dismay of all the ruling elites. The latter included the local Soviet bosses and the heads of their respective Communist parties, excluding President Askar Akaev who was the head of the Academy of Sciences of Kyrgyzstan. During the preindependence era, they ran their respective republics as totalitarian leaders carrying out the Soviet central government's instructions. The fall of the Soviet system made them all the leaders of their republics at a time when all the components of that system—including its leading ideology, Communism—were becoming totally discredited.

The fall of the mighty Soviet Union shook the entire Soviet society and paved the way for the surge of nationalism in all the former Soviet republics, including those of the Caucasus and Central Asia. By the force of realities, their leaders—formerly staunch supporters of Communism—suddenly became the firm proponents of nationalism. The discredited Communist ideology could no longer be their guiding ideology once it had no attractiveness for their peoples. Nor could it be so in the absence of its corresponding political system, the Soviet system. Furthermore, their shift to nationalism was in tune with the sudden emergence of nationalist sentiments long suppressed during the Russian and Soviet eras. It was therefore a means for the legitimization of their rule, which had been identified with all the ills of the Soviet era. Moreover, it was a necessity for creating a national consensus in order to unite the peoples of their countries and consolidate their shaken political system. Finally, the leaders of the eight newly independent states could not continue the Soviet-created closed political and social systems based on the Soviet command economy. That economy, which had been ailing in the last years of the Soviet era, began to fall apart in the postindependence era when Moscow suddenly stopped its economic assistance. The lack of adequate domestic resources to compensate for the loss of the Soviet-provided assistance in cash, fuel, and equipment paralyzed their economies. In such a situation, the Caucasian and CA leaders, who were facing a surge of nationalism and a demand for a radical break with the past, were unable to continue the Soviet totalitarian system without its corresponding economic and ideological bases.

As a result, the period following the fall of the Soviet Union has been somewhat different from the immediate Soviet era, but it has not been an era of democracy. Without a doubt, the postindependence era has not demonstrated a total break with the past either in form or content. In one way or another, the Caucasian and CA leaders have all established their regimes on the basis of the existing political machinery—that is, the inherited Soviet political system. They have kept the Soviet bureaucracy, a major component of the old system, in place almost intact. In practice, the newly established ruling nationalist parties are mainly the renamed Communist parties and run by their preindependence leadership. Other legal nationalist political parties have been formed by former senior members of the Soviet-era Communist parties who have close ties to the Caucasian and CA leaders or to their ruling parties. It is no surprise that they have formed docile opposition. The existing Communist parties are simply a fraction of the old ones, with no practical influence or any relevance to the political reality. Hence the legal political parties, which have dominated the postindependence life of the Caucasian and CA countries, have all continued the content and the basic structure of the old Communist parties, with minor differences in form as imposed by the new era.

The practical retention of the components of the preindependence political system has resulted in the continuity of the old undemocratic system in a different form. The preservation of the old bureaucracy and the political-party system has resulted in the survival of their corresponding political thinking, which is that of the highly centralized and undemocratic Soviet political system. The persistence of the old state-dominated economic system for the most part has maintained an economic basis suitable for the continuation of such a political system in a different form, because the Soviet economic system has fallen but the desired free-enterprise economy has yet to be created. The failure of the Caucasian and CA countries to create such an economy has forced them to revive the old economic system to the extent possible. Given the poor economic situation, this is a necessity to avoid a total economic collapse and mass unemployment, with predictably dire political consequences. In short, the existence of the old political apparatus and the remnants of the old economic system have created a suitable ground for the formation of a highly centralized and undemocratic political system—namely, an authoritarian system.

Authoritarianism has been a trend in the entire Caucasian and CA countries since their independence. However, their leaders have opted for that type of government at different points in time, and they have consolidated it at a different pace as necessitated by the concrete situation in their respective countries. Nevertheless, their political systems have from the very first day of independence shared certain authoritarian characteristics. Without exception, all the Caucasian and CA leaders have formed highly centralized states in which political power is concentrated in the hands of a president who rules like a tyrant accountable to no one. Strong presidential political systems have left no room for fully functional democratic institutions such as parliaments. The existing ones have become practically rubber stamps for their respective presidents, who control just about every aspect of life in their countries. Although the presidents have been elected or reelected through elections, they are all life-time presidents (with one exception—Armenia). In the case of Kazakhstan and Turkmenistan, their presidents have become life-time presidents through referenda. In other cases, the state machinery has ensured the reelection of the presidents by various means, including banning rival parties, disqualifying or intimidating rival candidates, the intimidation of voters, and ballot-stuffing. In such a situation, a multiparty system as a necessity for the free expression of political, economic, and social interests on the part of different interest groups has become an unaffordable political luxury. Unsurprisingly, free and fair elections as a democratic means for popular representation at the different levels of government and also as a means for ensuring a peaceful change of government have become a meaningless democratic concept, available on paper only. In practice, all positions at different levels of government are filled with progovernment appointees or with elected candidates whose elections are guaranteed through the manipulation of the electoral process.

A major component of authoritarianism has been a zero-tolerance policy toward meaningful political dissent in any form and any extent on the part of individuals or groups. Religious and nonreligious, including nationalist, groups and individual activists challenging the authority and the legitimacy of the ruling elites have all been targeted. As a rule, the main pretext for their suppression regardless of their political orientation has been, at least officially, the removal of the threat of Islamic fundamentalism. The ruling elites have all sought to take advantage of the prevailing antifundamentalist mood in the West and in some Middle-Eastern countries, a mood shared also by Russia to serve its interests in the region. In the predominantly Muslim CA countries and Azerbaijan, fundamentalists have been portrayed as the main source of threat to national security. In all the Caucasian and CA countries, other opposition groups have been suppressed on charges such as their destructive activities or their weakening or defaming of their respective political systems or presidents. Regardless of the pretext used, the Caucasian and CA governments have suppressed religious and nonreligious opposition groups or individuals through banning their activities altogether, disqualifying them from elections, imprisonment of their members and sympathizers, and official or unofficial physical elimination of their leading figures. In practice, they have only allowed progovernment political parties or docile political opposition. The latter consists of political parties that do not pose any short- or long-term threat to the legitimacy of their respective states. Finally, a ruthless security force ensures the compliance of all citizens with the wishes of the political elites. This is the continuation of a Soviet/Russian tradition dating back to Czarist Russia.

Against this general authoritarian background, there have been differences among the Caucasian and CA countries. In certain countries—Azerbaijan, Georgia, Turkmenistan, Tajikistan, and Uzbekistan—the elites opted for an outright authoritarian political system from the very first day of independence, even though their brands of authoritarianism differ in form and intensity. In the first two countries, the current presidents, Haidar Aliev and Edward Sheverdnadzhe, came to power in 1993 during civil wars, which lasted until 1994 and 1993, respectively. In both cases, ceasefire agreements ended the wars without addressing their root causes. The chaos and strong sense of insecurity as a result of civil wars and the practical independence of large parts of their countries (Nagorno Karbakh for Azerbaijan, and Abkhazia and South Ossetia for Georgia) severely weakened the authority, power, and legitimacy of their central governments. Added to this situation, the need for establishing law and order and revitalizing the devastated economy justified a high-handed government policy. It further strengthened the prevailing mood conducive for the creation of authoritarian regimes in Azerbaijan and Georgia.

The political life in these countries has been characterized by a variety of ills. They include the suppression of dissent and of political opposition parties, the absence of individual rights and freedoms, the manipulation of elections, an inefficient and corrupt bureaucracy, and a despotic government. In each country, the small ruling circle and their family members have monopolized the major political and economic positions. This is especially evident in the case of President

Aliev. Almost all of his family members, including his son, son-in-law, and brother, have occupied major influential positions since he rose to power.[2] Although some opposition parties still exist in Azerbaijan and Georgia, their regimes have practically excluded them from the political scene, leaving it secured for the ruling parties—the Yeni Azerbaijan [New Azerbaijan] and the Citizens' Union of Georgia, respectively.

In Tajikistan, the ruling elite's intolerance of the growing genuine opposition groups led to a devastating five-year civil war.[3] The opposition coalition, consisting of Islamic and secular groups formed by the non-Soviet elite, represented the deprived regions of Tajikistan, which have been traditionally out of the circles of power. The coalition won the 1992 presidential election, but its rule lasted only for a few months until a joint force of the Tajik Soviet elite and the Uzbek government removed them by military force late in 1992. That development escalated into a fully fledged, bloody civil war, which ended only when the two sides concluded a power-sharing arrangement as part of a peace accord in June 1977. As a result, the Tajik government legalized the members of the Tajik united opposition groups, which had fought against the central government for about five years. They were two secular groups, the Democratic Party of Tajikistan (DPR) and the Rastakhiz [Resurrection]; an Islamic group, the Islamic Renaissance Party (IRP); and a group advocating greater autonomy for Pamiri peoples of the Gorno-Badakhshan Autonomous region, the Lali Badakhshan. These political groups are now part of the ruling coalition. However, other small political opposition groups have remained banned and are treated harshly. In May 2001, the Tajik government sentenced to death two Tajiks identified only as "Islamic militants."[4]

Turkmenistan and Uzbekistan have been the most authoritarian countries of Central Asia. In both countries, presidential elections have been eliminated. Through referenda in the 1990s, the Turkmen president, Safarmorad Niyazov, was given life-time presidency, while the presidential term of the Uzbek president, Islam Karimov, was extended one more time. Their governments have pursued a policy of zero tolerance toward any type of political activity outside the pro-government one. Under the banner of fighting Islamic extremism (which has been very insignificant), the Uzbek government has banned, dissolved, or destroyed all independent and antigovernment groups with both religious and secular tendencies.[5] Its fear of a rapid expansion of political opposition in the first two years of independence when the country was unable to meet even its basic needs created a justification for an iron-fist policy. The rise of a political opposition, including Islamic groups, strengthened its resolve for pursuing that policy. Despite the end of the civil war in Tajikistan and the insignificance of the outlawed opposition groups, the Uzbek government has whitewashed its authoritarianism as a necessity for its fight against Islamic fundamentalism and extremism. While the Uzbek government has used the existence of some opposition groups as an excuse for suppressing dissent, the Turkmen government has done the same in the absence of such a potential threat. In fact, it has gone beyond the suppression of opposition groups to eliminate practically any type of political group and activity other than those related to the governing party. The cult of personality of President Safarmorad Niyazov has been the defining characteristic of the Turkmen authoritarianism since independence. This has turned Turkmenistan into an extreme case as its political system is taking a Stalinist form, which is a step further backward even from the last few decades of the Soviet Union.

In a comparative sense, Armenia, Kazakhstan, and Kyrgyzstan initially opted for a more democratic type of government. The Armenian government has been as undemocratic as its counterparts in the Caucasus and Central Asia in many ways, including in terms of abusing rights and freedoms of individuals. What has made it distinct from all others is its acceptance of changing guards at the presidential level. This has made it the only country in the two regions ruled by different presidents since independence who have left office according to the due process. Azerbaijan, Georgia, and Tajikistan have also had more than one president, but the presidents elected before the current ones were all forced out of office before finishing their terms. The other four countries have had the same president since independence. These differences aside, the two Armenian presidents since independence, Levond Ter-Petrosian and Robert Kocharian, have not governed their countries in a style very different from that of their counterparts in other Caucasian and CA countries. Arrest and imprisonment of opponents, including political rivals, have been the norm in Armenia. So too has been the manipulation of parliamentary elections in favor of the desired candidates.

In the early 1990s, Kazakhstan and Kyrgyzstan became known for their region as model countries where democratic values were taking hold. The control of society by the government and its security forces has been less significant than that in other Caucasian and CA countries, leaving room for a degree of free political life. To some extent, tolerance for political parties, including opposition ones, has existed since independence. A major reason for this situation has been the absence of political parties or influential individuals strong or potentially strong enough to pose a serious challenge to the Kazakh and Kyrgyz governments. In particular, extremist groups, whether secular or Islamic fundamentalist, have not existed in those countries. By and large, the political groups have been weak numerically and negligible politically. However, the more democratic sentiments in these countries have not excluded restrictions on the freedoms and rights of individuals and on the political activities of all the parties in one way or another. Efforts have been made to turn these parties into politically irrelevant groups. Various legal and practical restrictions have limited their participation in different elections (e.g., parliamentary and presidential) to ensure the election of the desired candidates. The worsening of the economic situation and the expansion of social discontent have gradually reduced the level of tolerance of political dissent in these countries and led to a more abusive approach toward their populations. Their leaders have gradually followed the lead of their counterparts in other CA and Caucasian countries in establishing authoritarianism. Kazakh President Nursultan Nazarbayev turned himself into the lifetime president of Kazakhstan late in the 1990s. Abuse of political activists, including their arrest and trial, under different pretexts including the weakening of presidency, defamation of leaders, or assassination attempts have become a common practice in these countries. In 2000, Topchubek Turgunaliev, the leader of a Kyrgyz opposition party called the Erkindik Party, was imprisoned on reportedly false charges of masterminding an assassination plot against President Askar Akaev.[6] In addition, tolerance for dissent within the ruling elite is also eroding. A recent noteworthy example is the imprisonment of Vice-President Feliks Kulov, which provoked an antigovernment demonstration in Kyrgyzstan in June 2000.[7] The continuation of this trend will certainly lead to the consolidation of authoritarianism in Kazakhstan and Kyrgyzstan.

A decade after independence, authoritarianism has become the dominant form of government in the entire Caucasus and Central Asia. Certain factors have created grounds for its rise and consolidation in the postindependence era. These can be divided into two major categories: the historical factors and the concrete situation in the postindependence era.

Without a doubt, the historical factors have played a major role in the rise of authoritarianism. Over the last two centuries, the process of social, political, and economic development in the Caucasus and Central Asia has prevented the creation of democracy as a form of government. By denying the opportunity for the foundation of democratic values and institutions, it has set grounds for the formation of consecutive undemocratic political systems ranging from totalitarianism to authoritarianism. About two centuries ago, the eight Caucasian and CA countries were incorporated into the Russian Empire, a highly centralized and despotic political system. Russia's annexation of these countries through wars and its ruthless suppression of their anti-Russian and independence movements in the first and a good part of the second half of the nineteenth century established violence against any type of dissent as the norm for government.[8] As an example, the Russian military crushed various anti-Russian movements in the Caucasus during the 30 years following the annexation of the Caucasus in the early nineteenth century.[9] The Russian government reinforced this violent "tradition" of dealing with dissent by imposition of its authoritarian form of government on Central Asia and the Caucasus. During their rule over those regions, Russian-appointed officials ran their countries as Russian provinces with impunity for more than a century. They derived their legitimacy from their subordination to the Russian central government in Moscow, to which they were accountable. This form of government was hostile to any type of manifestation of democracy and advocated an iron-fist approach to statecraft. Fear of government became the main means for ensuring the docility of the people all over Russia, and especially in its conquered and rebellious territories in the Caucasus and Central Asia. This despotic form of government excluded people from participation in the political process and was intolerant of any type of political opposition. With a great deal of success, the Russians suppressed all types of political activities that challenged the authority of their state, including political parties and movements and individual efforts to democratize those countries.

The 1917 Bolshevik Revolution overthrew the Russian Empire, only to replace it with an even more undemocratic political system. The Soviet elite imposed a totalitarian system of government on the entire Russian territory, including its Asian republics. During its over seven decades of rule, the Soviet central government in Moscow created a highly centralized and antidemocratic form of government in these republics. The main task of the republican governments was to carry out the instructions of the central government in Moscow, in all major aspects of life. The Soviet leaders continued the Tsarist tradition of appointing all the republican elite and virtually all of their officials with any significant influence, without any type of involvement of the people affected. The appointees' absolute loyalty to the political system, but not their competence and popularity, became the criterion for their appointment. Following the routine in the entire Soviet republic, the local bosses ruled over their respective republics like absolute monarchs, using democratic institutions (e.g., republican parliaments) as a rubber stamp only. This ceremonial function of the republican parliaments and that of the Soviet parliament in Moscow discredited parliament in general as a major institution on which a democratic political system should be based. It also simply eliminated the principle of accountability of political leaders and top officials to the parliamentary representatives of their people as a component of the republican political systems. Abuse of elections also discredited and weakened parliamentary tradition. Elections became meaningless processes through which the hand-picked loyal politicians received legitimacy by voters forced to cast their ballots for them.

Both the Soviet central government and its subordinate republican governments implemented a policy of zero tolerance toward dissent. This resulted in the stifling of all kinds of expression of opinions and political activities outside the framework of the dominant Communist party. To that end, Stalin executed millions of Soviet people, including Caucasians and Central Asians, in the 1930s and 1940s for their opposition to the Soviet regime. Many others were executed because of their opposition to particular government policies, such as the forced collectivization of agriculture.[10] Additionally, large scores of people including Communist party members and government officials at all levels were exiled, imprisoned, or sent to mental hospitals during the Soviet era. The police state created by the Soviet leaders sanctioned, encouraged, and institutionalized abuses by authorities at different levels of government. Such abuses were considered necessary for the continuation of the single-party Soviet regime. Moreover, like its predecessor, the Soviet regime did not allow the formation of a participatory political culture in which various political views could be represented through different political groups. The Soviet single-party system simply prevented by force the creation of any type of political, economic, or social-interest group advocating any idea other than those sanctioned by the Soviet Communist party. Besides, it did not recognize political and human rights of individuals whose lives were at the mercy of the Soviet regime.

At the time of independence, the existing political system—with its two centuries of antidemocratic heritage—became that of the newly established states of the Caucasus and Central Asia. Its antidemocratic guiding ideology, Communism, had disappeared, but the resulting ideological vacuum was not filled with democratic ideologies. Instead, the preindependence elites now ruling their respective independent republics simply continued the inherited preindependence political system minus its guiding ideology. Nationalism filled the ideological vacuum and became their states' ideology. Hence, authoritarianism—the Soviet totalitarian political system without its ideological objective of creating a superior Soviet nation—became the "natural" form of government for the new elites. In short, the postindependence Caucasian and CA countries were not built on qualitatively different values and practices that would justify and demand a totally different political system—that is, a democratic one, accountable to the people while encouraging and providing for their participation in the political process.

Apart from these historical factors, the specific situations in the Caucasus and Central Asia have contributed to the rise of authoritarianism in four different ways. The lack of a prodemocracy movement in these regions in the 1980s has been a major contributing factor. During the last decade of the Soviet Union, these regions were the least interested in the democratization of the Soviet political and social systems and in independence itself. There were hardly any significant independence or prodemocracy movements in their countries. In the Caucasus, Georgia was the most enthusiastic republic for independence, but its pro-independence movement was suppressed brutally by the Soviet military in 1989. Anti-Soviet movements existed in both Armenia and Azerbaijan, but they did not grow very much. In a comparative sense, Azerbaijan showed a little more enthusiasm for independence, as reflected in the rise of a nationalist party, the Azerbaijan Popular Front (APF). The two neighbors were involved in a bloody territorial dispute in the late 1980s until the fall of the USSR, which overshadowed other issues, including independence movements. In Central Asia, in 1989 the removal of a Kazakh as the head of Kazakhstan's Communist party and the appointment of a Russian from outside the republic to that position provoked antigovernment demonstrations. The Soviet government suppressed these mainly student demonstrations. Beyond these events, the eight Soviet republics remained more or less calm, with no major sign of a strong desire for independence and democracy. At the same time, other Soviet republics such as Ukraine and the three Baltic republics were engaged in almost daily activities toward those objectives. Consequently, independence did not put a demand on the leaders of the newly independent states of the Caucasus and Central Asia for a break with the past and the establishment of democratic political systems. In the absence of pressure from below for a change, those leaders did not feel obliged to work toward those ends. Authoritarianism became an unchallenged form of government for those states.

Authoritarianism has its roots also in the efforts of the Caucasian and CA elites to strengthen their rule. Upon independence, they inherited troubled countries, as the last few years of the Soviet regime were chaotic. Contrary to his intentions, the political and economic reforms of Mikhail Gorbachev did not address the shortcomings of the Soviet system. Rather, they weakened the pillars of Soviet political, economic, and social systems without addressing their deficiencies; the result was the worsening of them all. Furthermore, his insistence on the need for reforms questioned the validity of the Soviet leading ideology (Communism), which had long been introduced as a perfect ideology with a recipe for all imaginable problems. The reforms deteriorated the ailing economy of the Soviet Union and delegitimized its political system. Its sanctioning of a limited degree of personal and political freedom increased the expectations of people long suppressed through the denial of their basic rights and freedoms. No wonder if the political systems that the Caucasian and CA elites inherited from the Soviet era were weak and therefore vulnerable to any popular challenge. The sudden fall of the Soviet Union awakened nationalist sentiments and encouraged a desire for a change in the overall situation. In addition to this, the sudden deterioration of the economic situation, rising unemployment and poverty, and the widespread disruption in the distribution of basic necessities created major legitimacy challenges for the Caucasian and CA governments. Their inability to stop the economic decline of their countries and to meet the basic needs of their respective peoples endangered the stability and security of their states. Fear of the eruption of dissent because of a sudden fall in living standards made the Caucasian and CA leaders question the wisdom of democracy for their countries. Knowing their inability to address the expanding economic and social problems in the short-run, the leaders found the establishment of a police state functioning through a highly centralized despotic government as the only viable option for them. Hence, authoritarianism became a necessary form of government to ensure the survival of their newly independent states and to guarantee their status and power in the new era.

In addition, authoritarianism is a response to the emerging dissent in the Caucasian and CA countries. Although there are differences among them with respect to their economic and social situations, all of them have experienced major social and economic difficulties since independence. Theoretically, the situation should have been better in the energy-producing countries of Azerbaijan, Kazakhstan, and Turkmenistan. However, various factors have prevented the full development of these countries' oil and natural-gas resources.[11] Suffice it to state that a decade after independence, their energy exports are still insignificant and do not generate adequate income to satisfy their growing needs. Their large and growing foreign debt has demonstrated their financial inability. As a result, the economic situation of the three energy producers is not fundamentally different from their non-energy-producing neighbors. Nor will it be qualitatively different as long as their energy exports remain limited. The economic deterioration in all the Caucasian and CA countries has contributed to the rise of various social problems, including poverty, drug-addiction, and drug-trafficking. Added to these, the worsening economic problems have contributed to the rise of political dissent.

The form, extent, and threatening nature of the political dissent vary from country to country. As discussed earlier, the Caucasus has been an especially worrisome example for the countries of the two regions. Instability has taken an extremely violent form in Azerbaijan and Georgia, where active independence movements exist. The Azeri–Armenian territorial dispute over Nagorno Karabakh began in 1988 when all the involved parties were part of the Soviet Union. The dispute outlived the Soviet Union and continued when Azerbaijan and

Armenia gained independence in 1991, at which time their bloody war had entered its fourth year. A ceasefire was negotiated in 1994, which ended the war, but not the dispute itself. The unresolved territorial conflict has the potential to reemerge in the form of an active war. In this case, it will not only pit Armenia and Azerbaijan against each other, but will open grounds for the involvement of regional and nonregional countries in support of one side or another. In their neighboring Georgia, dissatisfaction with the status quo took the form of civil war at the time of independence. The breakaway regions of South Ossetia and Abkhazia fought a bloody war with the Georgian government which lasted until late 1992 and 1993, respectively, when a ceasefire terminated the war while not resolving its root causes. For this simple reason, war could resume at any time. The continued on-and-off war of pro-President Gamsakhurdia forces with the Georgian government since 1993 has further increased instability in Georgia. In short, all the Caucasian leaders have experienced major destabilizing events in their own countries. They have also been affected in one way or another by instability in their neighboring countries, such as in Russia with regard to Chechnya. It could easily expand to their countries because of strong ethnic and historical ties. Fear of such a scenario has convinced them all of the merits of an iron-fist policy. Their hope is that such a policy can help them both contain destabilizing forces within their territory and prevent the spillover of instability from their neighbors. Not surprisingly, they have all spent large funds on their military and security forces. In 1998, for example, Armenia's and Azerbaijan's military expenditure accounted, respectively, for 3.6% and 2.7% of their GDP.[12] The heavy burden of such expenditure can better be understood if it is seen in terms of overall government spending. In 2001, for example, Azerbaijan increased its military spending to $111 million, equal to 13% of all budget expenditures for that year.[13]

The CA leaders have had various reasons for their concern about the emergence and expansion of instability in their countries. Its existence in violent and extensive forms in the Caucasus has raised concern about the possibility of such a scenario in Central Asia among its leaders. Undoubtedly, in comparison to the Caucasus where all its countries have been struggling with large-scale violent dissent in different forms, Central Asia has experienced limited politically motivated violence since 1991. So far, the most alarming case in that region has been Tajikistan. The five-year civil war in Tajikistan not only frightened the Tajik leaders and made them fearful about the future stability of their state, it sent a chill all over their region. Prior to the conclusion of the peace treaty in June 1997, there was a fear that the civil war could expand to the entire region because of the regional ethnic makeup. In addition, the fact that the growth of dissatisfaction with the status quo helped the expansion of the Tajik opposition forces to such an extent as to challenge the authority of their government made all the CA leaders concerned. The existence of similar dissatisfaction in the other four regional countries made the duplication of the same scenario in those countries a distinct possibility, even though opposition groups were small in number and very weak and insignificant everywhere outside Tajikistan.[14] In particular, the Uzbeks were fearful of the possibility of the spillover of the Tajik war into their country. Certain factors made this quite feasible, including their sharing a long border with Tajikistan, their having a large Tajik minority, and their strong ethnic and religious ties with the Tajiks. It is no wonder that they became the main regional ally of the Tajik government in its war against the opposition forces. Sharing the same concerns, other regional countries (e.g., Kazakhstan and Kyrgyzstan) also helped the Tajiks in one way or another.[15] Despite scattered violations of the Tajik peace treaty, peace has held in Tajikistan to this date. Nevertheless, the main causes of the civil war (e.g., regional disparity and the monopolization of the power by the Soviet elite) have yet to be fully addressed. As a result, worries about the resumption of the civil war still justifiably exist.

The Tajik civil war strengthened the trend in certain CA countries toward authoritarianism. To preempt the emergence of a strong opposition force, which could challenge their legitimacy, the governments of Turkmenistan and Uzbekistan have suppressed all political groups other than the ruling ones. In the case of Turkmenistan, apart from a fear of future threat, the existence of a multiparty system does not fit with the cult of personality of President Niyazov in any case. As mentioned before, the Uzbek government was particularly concerned about the duplication of the Tajik civil war in Uzbekistan. Nevertheless, it clearly exaggerated the threat of opposition groups and especially the Islamic ones to justify the suppression of all the political groups falling outside the pro-establishment realm of political activity. During the Tajik civil war, Kazakhstan and Kyrgyzstan did not face a growing opposition, nor did they have any major radical group whether religious or secular. These two factors resulted in their more liberal approach to their political parties, including their opposition, which were too weak to pose any threat.

Apart from the Tajik civil war, the rise of instability in the Ferghana Valley has created a major concern in all of Central Asia. Instability in the Ferghana Valley has taken the form of an armed movement whose extent and threat is a matter of disagreement. In particular, this situation has been an immediate security threat for the three regional countries sharing the valley—namely, Kyrgyzstan, Tajikistan, and Uzbekistan. The Uzbek part of the valley has been the stronghold of Uzbek religious organizations since 1991. The Uzbek government has exaggerated its strength and sought to introduce them as a major security threat to its country and that of the entire region. Of course, there have been radical Islamic groups in there, but they have been too small and weak to challenge the authority of the Uzbek regime. The parts of the Ferghana Valley located in Kyrgyzstan and Tajikistan were not the troubled areas until recently. Since late 1999, the entire valley has become a source of concern for the three regional countries. It has become a scene of on-and-off military operations between the security forces of Kyrgyzstan, Tajikistan, and Uzbekistan on the one hand, and two types of armed groups on the other. One of these is a radical Islamic group called the Islamic Movement of Uzbekistan (IMZ). Reportedly, it seeks political objectives in the region ranging from the overthrow of the three regional governments sharing the valley to the creation of a united Islamic state in the valley. Despite the Uzbek government's claims, the group is still too small and too weak to be a major security threat, although its small-scale hit-and-run armed operations have become a source of threat to the local government forces. Nor is there any indication of its ability to grow rapidly. Nevertheless, it could become a major security threat in the future if the economic situation continues to worsen in the three countries sharing the Ferghana Valley. In such a situation, the growing dissatisfaction among the regional people will create a suitable environment for the expansion of antigovernment views, including radical ones.

International drug-traffickers form the other armed group in the Ferghana Valley. The latter have been the major source of threat for the three regional countries and, in fact, for all of Central Asia. Their on-and-off fighting turned into a full-fledged war in 2000, which lasted for many months and resulted in heavy casualties for the regional and especially Kyrgyz security forces.[16] Being divided among three regional countries, instability in the valley could directly destabilize Kyrgyzstan, Tajikistan, and Uzbekistan. Factors such as the ethnic makeup of Central Asia could help spread this instability to Kazakhstan and Turkmenistan. The traffickers have resorted to military operations to secure a safe corridor for their "trade" from Afghanistan to Europe through the Central Asian countries. These countries have gradually replaced Iran, which provides the shortest link between Afghanistan and Europe via Turkey, as the main drug route. The fortification of Iran's border with Afghanistan and the imposition of the death penalty for traffickers have sharply reduced the use of the Iranian route by drug-traffickers. In search of an alternative route, they have selected Central Asia. As a land link between Afghanistan and Russia through which narcotics are smuggled into Europe, that region is a "natural" route for large-scale smuggling operations. The lack of experience and resources of its security forces to deal with such operations, on the one hand, and Russia's growing market for narcotics, on the other, have made Central Asia the preferred route for drug barons. They have resorted to violence to neutralize the efforts of certain Central Asian countries—namely, Kyrgyzstan, Tajikistan, and Uzbekistan—to stop their "trade." Their military operation has sought to secure a safe corridor between Afghanistan, their producer of narcotics, and Kazakhstan, their gate to Russia.

Like any other phenomenon, there are both internal and external factors responsible for the expansion of drug-trafficking via Central Asia. As an internal factor, the poor economic situation and poverty in this region have helped drug-traffickers recruit locals to conduct their operation. However, the main root of this operation should be found in the worsening situation in Afghanistan. After over two decades of civil war, the prevailing chaos in that country has turned it into the largest producer of opium and heroin worldwide. The growing international market for narcotics creates strong incentives for international drug-traffickers to protect their lucrative trade at any price. Their extensive financial resources enable them to raise "armies" in Central Asia, consisting of locals and others such as Russians. The long period of instability in Afghanistan and the dominance of the fundamentalist Taliban over about 90% of that country, which lasted until November 2001, have directly contributed to the expansion of illicit-drug operations. It was no secret that the Taliban tolerated, if not encouraged, the cultivation of narcotic plants and the production of opium and heroin, for example, in their territories.[17] Despite the fall of the Taliban, there is no indication of an end to the drug production and drug-trafficking, as the weakness of the Afghan interim government and the persistence of the chaotic situation in most parts of Afghanistan have ensured the continuity of these evils. In short, the armed confrontation between the international drug-traffickers and the regional security forces has been a clear evidence for the destabilizing nature of international drug-trafficking for Central Asia.

Besides internal factors, certain external factors have also contributed to the emergence of authoritarianism in the Caucasus and Central Asia. Instability in the proximity of these regions has been a major contributing factor. Sharing common borders and having ethnic, religious, and historical ties with Afghanistan, China, and Russia, chronic instability to a varying extent in these countries has created the fear of their expansion into these regions. The factors making them vulnerable to threats from inside have also made them vulnerable to external threats. The situation is therefore ripe in these two regions for a rapid expansion of instability from their troubled neighbors, which are confronting different types of destabilizing forces.

The prolonged civil war in Afghanistan endangered the stability of its neighboring CA countries, in two ways. First, the Afghan-based drug-trafficking has destabilized part of Central Asia and created the potential for it expanding to other parts, as discussed earlier. Second, the continuation of the Afghan civil war created the possibility for its spillover into its neighboring CA countries. While civil war in the form of war between the Northern Alliance and the Taliban no longer exists, the civil-war atmosphere has continued in the form of rivalry between and among local warlords, and also in the form of fighting over territories between Pashtun warlords. In the absence of strong central government, the situation is ripe for the resumption of civil war all over the country. Among other factors, ethnic rivalry and the presence of regional and nonregional powers in Afghanistan are contributing factors to this situation.

Afghanistan has been unstable for over two decades. The Soviet-backed coup of 1978 triggered a civil war in Afghanistan. It drastically expanded in 1980 when the Soviet Union dispatched about 100,000 troops to that country in support of its weak Afghan protégé.

The war took the form of fighting between several Afghan Mujahedin groups and the joint forces of the Soviet troops and pro-Soviet Afghan central government. However, the 1989 withdrawal of the Soviet forces and the fall of the pro-Soviet regime in 1992 did not end the civil war. Rather, they only served to provoke changing alliances among the Afghan Mujahedin groups and to lower the intensity of war for a while. The rise of the Taliban in 1994 worsened the situation not only for war-torn Afghanistan, but also for its neighboring regions. Despite its control of about 90% of the Afghan territory, with a few exceptions (i.e., Pakistan, Saudi Arabia, the UAE, and Turkmenistan) the international community recognized the ousted government of President Rabani as the only legal Afghan government, which lasted until the formation of the Afghan interim government in late 2001. Gathered under the umbrella of the Northern Alliance, the pro-president forces fought against the Taliban from the mid-1990s until the latter's demise in November 2001. The Taliban's rule over Afghanistan and its war with the Northern Alliance forces not only prolonged the devastation of Afghanistan, it prepared the ground for the expansion of instability from Afghanistan into its neighboring regions. This possibility has always been a major concern for the regional countries, but the emergence of the Taliban added a new dimension to it. The group had regional ambitions and sought to export its fundamentalist views to the countries in its proximity. While the extent of its ability to achieve its ambitions was a matter of disagreement, there was no doubt about its harboring terrorists from different regional and non-regional countries in its territory.

The expansion of fundamentalism to the Caucasian and CA countries by the Taliban was a long-term concern. In spite of the disappearance of the Taliban as a major political force, if the economic situation does not improve and if corruption and abuses of human rights continue and expand, the inevitable rise of mass opposition in these countries will prepare the ground for a rapid expansion of extremist ideologies, including fundamentalist ones, which still exist both in Afghanistan and in Central Asia. Fundamentalists, including those who subscribe to Taliban-like ideologies, could, and probably will, seek to take advantage of such opportunities to export their subversive ideologies. While in power, the Taliban had only a limited opportunity for influencing other countries, as evident in its negligible influence in southern CIS countries. There has been little evidence of fundamentalism as a political movement in Central Asia and the Caucasus, despite statements to the contrary by certain governments, such as those of Kyrgyzstan, Tajikistan, and Uzbekistan. The Russian government has claimed the active participation of the Taliban in the war in Chechnya. If it is true, it should should have been very limited and not a determining factor in the pace of war, as the Taliban did not have the resources to project its power in an extensive manner over 2,500 kilometers from Afghanistan. The activities of religious groups, including fundamentalist ones, in the Ferghana Valley have been far less significant than claimed.

As a potential source of security threat, instability in China has also been a concern for most of the CA leaders and a factor contributing to their shift to authoritarianism. Neighboring Kazakhstan, Kyrgyzstan, and Tajikistan, China's Xinjiang Province has been experiencing instability for at least a decade.[18] Unlike other parts of China, its inhabitants are predominantly of Turkic origin, consisting of Central Asian ethnic groups—mainly Kazakhs, Uyghurs (Uighurs), and, to a lesser extent, Kyrgyz. Having strong ethnic ties with their neighboring Kazakhstan and Kyrgyzstan, these ethnic minorities, dominated by local ethnic Chinese have long been dissatisfied with their status in China. Against this background, the independence of their CA neighbors served as a catalyst and further encouraged their nationalist sentiments. Especially since the fall of the Soviet Union in 1991, they have resorted to a variety of anti-Chinese political activities demanding either independence or reunification with their kin in Kazakhstan through peaceful or violent means.[19] Facing this threatening situation, China has resorted to an iron-fist policy to contain its Turkic population through mass arrests, imprisonment, and execution of activists. For example, 190 Uyghurs were reportedly executed on political charges during the period 1997–99.[20] These harsh measures have enabled the Chinese government to control the situation and eliminate the immediate threat of separation of Xinjiang. Yet they have failed to uproot the anti-Chinese movements and to eliminate the nationalist aspirations of China's Turkic minorities. The secession of Xinjiang from China is a remote possibility in the foreseeable future, but there is no doubt that the separatist movements will continue in one form or another—namely, peaceful or violent. Such movements will inevitably awaken nationalist sentiments in neighboring CA countries, with unpredictable implications for those countries. The existence of strong support for China's Uyghurs among their kin in Kazakhstan leaves no doubt about the possibility of the rise of nationalist movements among them, as reflected in a recent event. In June 2001, the murder of Dilbirim Samsakova, a Kazakhstani Uyghur activist, in the town of Qapshaghay in Almaty Oblast brought about 1,000 Uyghurs from Almaty and also from neighboring Kyrgyzstan to her funeral.[21]

As a feasible scenario, worsening ties between China and its neighboring CA countries could be another source of security threat. Needless to say, this is an undesirable scenario for the CA governments, given China's strength and its rise as a major global power with historical claims to parts of Kazakhstan and Kyrgyzstan. Since 1991, fear of escalation of conflicts between the two sides over territorial disputes along their joint borders and on ethnic issues in Xinjiang has resulted in efforts on both sides to reach a common understanding.[22] Leaving ideological disputes apart, the territorial claims created grounds for skirmishes along the joint Sino-Soviet borders in the 1960s.[23] In the post-Soviet era, Kazakhstan and Kyrgyzstan, on the one hand, and China, on the other, have made efforts to keep their joint borders calm and tension-free, since both sides need a long period of peace to develop their respective economies. Confidence-building measures such as pulling back military forces from the border lines have removed the possibility of a sudden escalation of border disputes into military conflicts, but they have not settled the old problems once and for all.[24] In some cases, the agreements reached between the two sides since 1991 have created internal strife. For instance, the demarcation of China and Kyrgyzstan based on their 1996 agreement, which began in June 2001, met with major opposition in Kyrgyzstan's parliament. The parliament called on President Akaev to halt the demarcation and to abjure the agreement, declaring the 1996 agreement to be a sellout of Kyrgyz territory.[25] The agreement provided for ceding 125,000 hectares of Kyrgyz territory to China.[26]

As a major source of threat to the stability of the Caucasus, instability in Russia has also served as an external factor encouraging authoritarianism in that region. The fall of the Soviet Union not only led to the independence of its republics, but awakened nationalist fervor among various ethnic minorities in Russia. The most well-known case has been Chechnya, a territory in defiance of the Russian central government since 1991.[27] The conflict has now taken the form of an undeclared war of attrition, which receives very limited attention worldwide. The massive amount of news coverage given to that region began to disappear a few months after the Russian military entered Chechnya's capital, Grozny, in early 2000. Despite this lack of interest, the growing instability in Russia's Caucasian republic of Chechnya is a serious threat to the stability of the entire Caucasus, a region prone to instability for a wide range of political, economic, and social reasons.

The massive 1999 military operation of the Russian government sought to end the independence of Chechnya and restore Russian sovereignty over its breakaway republic.[28] The iron-fist policy of the Russian government helped its military capture Grozny, but it failed to end the civil war in the Northern Caucasus. In fact, that military "victory" only worsened the situation in Chechnya. Using its military might, Russia won a classic war against the Chechen rebels, who were unable to match Moscow in terms of weapons and personnel. Unable to defend major cities, including Grozny, with their mainly light weapons, the rebels left them and spread out into the countryside from where they have since imposed a costly and humiliating war of attrition on the Russian military. Instead of confronting the heavily armed Russian forces in their urban strongholds, the Chechen rebels have resorted to small-scale hit-and-run operations, inflicting constant casualties on those forces while damaging their military hardware. This is a type of war that the Russians cannot possibly win. They experienced it first-hand during their 1994–96 military campaign in Chechnya, which ended in their humiliating tolerance of Chechnya's independence. They also experienced it in Afghanistan in the 1980s, where they lost a nine-year war against the Mujahedin groups. If the recent history of their military engagement in Chechnya is any indication, the Russians should not expect a different result in the Northern Caucasus.

The Russian military operation in Chechnya has failed to achieve its main objective. The operation and the real or alleged war crimes committed during its course have secured worldwide condemnations for the Kremlin while failing to ensure the docility of the breakaway republic. In the postoperation period, the expansion of the Chechen rebels' military activities against the Russian forces has been a clear proof of Russia's inability to exert full control over Chechnya. Scattered news coming out of the republic as well as the Russian military's own accounts of the situation suggest that Russia has been tolerating heavy casualties in this period. It is even argued that these casualties have been heavier than the ones inflicted on Russia during its massive operation to capture Grozny.

Russia's military campaign has also failed to stabilize the Northern Caucasus. Chechnya is not only unstable, but its instability is actually expanding to other parts of that region. Russia's republics of Dagestan and Ingushetia are gradually showing signs of tension. This is only partly due to the expansion of the war from Chechnya to these republics, reflected in cross-border fighting and attacks by Chechen rebels on the Russian forces stationed there. Hosting large numbers of Chechen refugees, these predominately non-Russian republics with ethnic, religious, and historical ties with Chechnya have raised their dissatisfaction with Moscow's handling of the Chechen conflict. In the 1990s, there was a clear pro-Chechen mood among the people of Ingushetia and Dagestan.[29] In addition to the expression of discontent by their peoples, their political leaders, including their presidents, have also echoed their disapproval of the Russian policy toward Chechnya. Late in 2000, for instance, the president of Inghueshia raised his voice against the Russian military operation in Chechnya for its hardship on the civilians, leading to their influx into his republic where thousands of Chechens were living as refugees in difficult conditions.[30] The worsening economic situation in those republics has already created grounds for the rise of popular dissent, which could also take the form of independence movements. The existence of such a movement in their neighboring Chechnya makes that scenario a feasible one.

Given the social roots of its independence movement, instability will likely continue in Chechnya. Factors such as the ethnic and religious makeup of the three republics of the Northern Caucasus and their economic deterioration are contributing to the growth of instability in that region. This instability may well engulf the entire Caucasus for a wide range of reasons, including ethnic, religious, and historical ties between the northern and southern Caucasians. The existence of destabilizing forces in Armenia, Azerbaijan, and Georgia, on the one hand, and the grievances of their populations with the past and present Russian policies, on the other, will likely further contribute to the realization of such a scenario. After a decade of repeated military operations, it should by now be clear to the Russians that there is no military solution to the Chechen conflict. As Chechnya is part of

Russia, the Russian government's efforts to contain the Chechen separatist movement and to restore its control over Chechnya is understandable and justifiable. However, its resort to military means to end the civil war, coupled with its refusal to seek a political solution to the conflict in the interests of maintaining Russia's sovereignty over Chechnya and its territorial integrity, will likely deepen the conflict and, moreover, contribute to its spillover into the entire Caucasus.

In short, instability in the countries bordering the Caucasus and Central Asia has created fear among their governments. Given the declining economic situation and the growing social dissatisfaction, these countries are prone to a rapid expansion of instability. The existence of a variety of social, cultural, and historical commonalties between their peoples and their neighbors has made them sensitive to political upheavals in neighboring countries, which could expand to their countries. As discussed in Chapter 5, this fear has led them conclude security agreements with Russia and China, two neighboring countries with troubled territories bordering their countries. Appreciating their vulnerability, the CA and Caucasian governments have also seen merits in authoritarianism. They have used it as a means for preventing the rise and expansion of unauthorized nationalist and/or radical sentiments in response to the situation in neighboring countries hosting their ethnic or religious brothers and sisters.

NOTES

1. For an analysis of the Gorbachev reforms, see Ben Eklof, *Soviet Briefing: Gorbachev and the Reform Period* (Boulder, CO: Westview Press, 1989).

2. Hooman Peimani, *The Caspian Pipeline Dilemma: Political Games and Economic Losses* (Westport, CT: Praeger, 2001), 86.

3. For detailed information on the various factors contributing to the Tajik civil war and its conclusion, see Hooman Peimani, *Regional Security and the Future of Central Asia: The Competition of Iran, Turkey, and Russia* (Westport, CT: Praeger, 1998), 29–30, 56–57.

4. "Newsline," REF/RL, 13 June 2001.

5. Peimani, *Regional Security and the Future of Central Asia*, 29.

6. "Newsline," REF/RL, 4 September 2000.

7. "Newsline," REF/RL, 13 June 2000.

8. For an account on the process of incorporation of the Caucasus and Central Asia into Russia, see Document Publishing Unit, "A Glance at the History of the Northeastern Borders (From Sarakhs to Caspian)—Part One," *Majelieh-e Motaellat-e Asyaie Markazi va Ghafghaz* [*Central Asia and the*

Caucasus Review] (Tehran), 1, No. 1 (Summer 1992), 231–242; Document Publishing Unit, "A Glance at the History of the Northeastern Borders (From Sarakhs to Caspian)—Part Two," *Majelieh-e Motaellat-e Asyaie Markazi va Ghafghaz* [*Central Asia and the Caucasus Review*] (Tehran), 1, No. 2 (Autumn 1992), 259–280.

9. A major rebellion against the Russians was led by Sheikh Shamil, which created major security problem for the Russians for about 30 years. See Zekrollah Mohammadi, " Sheikh Shamil: The Leader of the Uprising of the Caucasian People against the Czars," *Majelieh-e Motaellat-e Asyaie Markazi va Ghafghaz* [*Central Asia and the Caucasus Review*] (Tehran), 2, No. 3 (Winter 1994), 15–50.

10. For an account on the Stalin era, see Geoffrey Hosking, *A History of the Soviet Union* (London: Fontana Press, 1985), 149–226.

11. For detailed information on the factors that prevented the full development of the Caucasian and Central Asian fossil-energy industry, see Peimani, *The Caspian Pipeline Dilemma.*

12. UNDP, *Human Development Report 2000* (New York: Oxford University Press, 2000), 215.

13. "Azerbaijan to Increase Military Spending," REF/RL, 9 March 2001.

14. Peimani, *Regional Security and the Future of Central Asia.*

15. Ibid., 66–67.

16. Hooman Peimani, "Drug-Trafficking in the Ferghana Valley and Instability in Central Asia," *The Times of Central Asia* (Bishkek), 2 November 2000.

17. Hooman Peimani, "Has the Taliban Regime Eradicated Opium Production," *Central Asia–Caucasus Analyst* (11 April 2001).

18. For details about the economic and geographical importance of Xinjiang for China, see Mohammad-Javad Omidvarniya, "A Review of the Natural Geography of the Xinjiang Uygur Autonomous Region," *Majelieh-e Motaellat-e Asyaie Markazi va Ghafghaz* [*Central Asia and the Caucasus Review*] (Tehran), 2, No. 1 (Summer 1993), 131–150.

19. Peimani, *The Caspian Pipeline Dilemma*, 48–49.

20. Glimpse of a Troubled Land, *The Economist*, 1 May 1999, 59.

21. "Uighur Activist Found Murdered in Kazakhstan," REF/RL, 13 June 2001.

22. For an account on the overall situation in Xinjinag and China's policy toward Central Asia, see John Calabrese, "China's Policy Towards Central Asia: Renewal and Accommodation," *Eurasian Studies* (Ankara), 16 (Autumn-Winter 1999), 75–98; see also Mohammad Javad Omidvarniya, "A Review of the Natural Geography of the Xinjiang Uyghur Autonomous Region," *Majelieh-e Motaellat-e Asyaie Markazi va Ghafghaz* [*Central Asia and the Caucasus Review*] (Tehran), 1, No. 2 (Summer 1993), 131–150.

23. For information on the Sino-Soviet conflicts, including their border skirmishes, see Nicholas V. Riasanovsky, *A History of Russia*, 4th ed. (New York: Oxford University Press, 1984).

24. Peimani, *Regional Security and the Future of Central Asia*, 67–68.

25. "Kyrgyz Parliament Calls on President to Disavow Border Accord," REF/RL, 16 June 2001.

26. Ibid.

27. For details on the factors behind the Chechen independence movement, see Musa al-Reza Vahidi, "Russia and the Crisis in the Northern Caucasus," *Majelieh-e Motaellat-e Asyaie Markazi va Ghafghaz [Central Asia and the Caucasus Review]* (Tehran), 28 (Winter 2000), 11–26.

28. For an account on the reasons behind Russia's military operation in Chechnya in 1999, see Nasser Saghafi-Ameri, "Editorial Note," *Majelieh-e Motaellat-e Asyaie Markazi va Ghafghaz [Central Asia and the Caucasus Review]* (Tehran), 28 (Winter 2000), 7–10; see also Vahidi, "Russia," 11–26.

29. Robert D. Blackwill, Rodric Braithwaite, and Akihiko Tanaka, "Russia's National Interests," *Majelieh-e Motaellat-e Asyaie Markazi va Ghafghaz [Central Asia and the Caucasus Review]* (Tehran), 23 (Fall 1998), 54.

30. "Signs of Discontent," *The Times of Central Asia* (Bishkek), 14 October 2000, 8.

5

Worrisome Trends

The first decade of independence has been very difficult for the three Caucasian and five CA countries. The first few years of their independence were extremely hard for their peoples, as they were experiencing a sudden collapse of their economies and fast-declining living standards. It was also very troublesome for their leaders, who were facing an ever-increasing number of difficulties of a political, economic, and social nature at a time when they were not prepared. In addition to this lack of preparedness, several other factors convinced many of them of the merits of authoritarianism right after independence, while over time the same factors have persuaded others to follow suit. Thus, authoritarianism in various forms and extents has become the prevailing type of government in the Caucasus and Central Asia a decade after independence. This type of government has been intended to help the eight states curb existing threats to their stability. Also, it has been intended to eliminate others or at least prevent them from developing into major ones. Yet the history of the first decade of independence has provided ample evidence that authoritarianism is not a solution to the Caucasian and CA transitional problems. For one, it has not secured the objective of curbing instability in certain countries (e.g., Georgia and Azerbaijan), nor has it achieved the goal of preventing the forces of instability from emerging in others (e.g., Uzbekistan). If the recent history is any indication, authoritarianism has actually been a contributing factor to the gradual emergence of popular dissent and instability. Given the current dismal economic situation and bleak prospects for the future, the consolidation and continuation of this form of government will inevitably pave the way for the rise and expansion of instability in different forms in the Caucasian and CA countries, with dire consequences for all of them. Various factors have provided suitable grounds for the instigation of civil wars in many of these countries, including the existence of large minorities in each country, which is a very probable and realistic form of instability for them. For a variety of reasons, such wars will have the potential to escalate to interstate wars pitting two neighbors against each other. The same reasons could also further escalate such wars to regional wars engaging most, if not all, countries of the Caucasus or Central Asia in a destructive military confrontation. The existence of certain regional (Iran, China, Turkey and Russia) and nonregional (United States) powers with long-term interests in these two regions could lead to their intentional or unintentional involvement in any type of future war in there. Such wars will have not only dire consequences for the security of those regions, but a major negative implication for the security of the international system.

RISE OF INSTABILITY AND ITS EXPANSION: A LIKELY TREND

The postindependence era has been one of decline in the newly independent states of the Caucasus and Central Asia. As in other ex-Soviet republics, the poor economic performance has lowered the living standards of the populations of the eight Caucasian and CA countries to different extents and depths. Without a doubt, there are differences among these countries in terms of their level of economic capabilities, resources, and potential for growth. Nevertheless, despite these differences there is no sign of a change for the better in their situations in the near future. The worsening economic and social situations have been contributing to the creation of a potentially dangerous political environment in the eight countries. Unless the current declining trend stops, the increasing multidimensional difficulties will surely provide grounds for the rise of extensive and long-term instability in various forms. Instability may begin in the form of peaceful expression of economic or political demands taking the shape of activities such as demonstrations and strikes, only to escalate to widespread antigovernment activities, including violent ones. The rise of popular dissent of a violent nature is the likely form of expression of political opposition to the status quo in those Caucasian and CA countries where the ruling elites have simply eliminated any opportunity for peaceful expression of dissatisfaction. Yet, in practice, this scenario will not be confined to them only, since all the Caucasian and CA countries have resorted to a high-handed policy toward their populations, either from the day of independence or a while after. The governments of those few countries (Kazakhstan and Kyrgyzstan) with a limited degree of tolerance for political freedom and political activities will most probably resort to outright violence against political opposition if this grows to the extent that could endanger governmental stability.

History is full of examples proving that violence is at best a short-term "solution" for the troubled states facing an opposition challenging their legitimacy. The use of force could silence popular dissent for a while, but it cannot eliminate its economic, social, and political roots. For that matter, unless the Caucasian and CA governments aim at resolving the root causes of social and political dissent, first and foremost by reviving their falling economies, authoritarianism in itself cannot guarantee their security and stability. Far from achieving those objectives, it will certainly contribute to the expansion of popular discontent among their respective peoples. More importantly, it will help radicalize their dissatisfied peoples, making them inclined to resort to violence. This is the likely form of expression of dissent at a time when peaceful dissent is out of the question. As popular dissatisfaction is growing in all the eight Caucasian and CA countries, the emerging antigovernment groups or movements, regardless of their insignificant numerical strength at the beginning, will likely expand rapidly. Needless to say, such developments will have a dangerous impact on the stability of the troubled Caucasian and CA countries, which need years of peace to tackle their numerous problems.

Rise of popular political dissent is not an unexpected scenario for the ex-Soviet republics. With perhaps only one exception (Estonia), all these republics have experienced a large number of economic, social, and political difficulties since their independence. In fact, even the most industrialized, technologically advanced, and prosperous ex-Soviet republics—namely, Russia and the Ukraine—have faced serious and extensive political opposition, challenging the authority and the legitimacy of their rulers. The case of Russia is especially alarming, as it has included prolonged armed and violent opposition with secessionist objective in its Caucasian region in addition to the emergence of hundreds of opposition political groups and parties elsewhere. The existence of political dissent is therefore not a peculiar characteristic of the Caucasian and CA countries. Nor is it a negative sign *per se*. On the contrary, in democratic societies political opposition is a sign of political health and a guarantee against the abuse of power by the rulers, whose power is limited by many laws and regulations. However, in the case of the eight Caucasian and CA countries, the absence of a democratic political system and the growing intolerance for political opposition even in the so-called democratic ones (i.e., Kazakhstan and Kyrgyzstan) make the rise and expansion of opposition groups a recipe for political disaster. In the absence of a democratic framework for the expression of different and opposite political views, the suppression of any such views from outside the government-sanctioned circle will pave the way for the rise of extremist ideologies. Repression and the absence of the possibility of a peaceful change of governments discredit political groups that advocate moderate ideologies and aim at reforming governments through peaceful means such as elections. In such a situation, radical views supporting a fundamental change in the political system through violence gain legitimacy and popularity as the only feasible way to change the undesired political system. Hence authoritarianism will contribute to and accelerate the radicalization of the dissatisfied Caucasian and CA peoples. Contrary to its objective of ensuring stability through the suppression of all unauthorized ideas and programs, it will destabilize their respective countries by providing grounds for the rise of extremist politics and political groups.

EMERGENCE OF EXTREMISM:
A RESPONSE TO THE DETERIORATING SITUATION

Historically, political extremism reflects the total dissatisfaction of a segment of the population with the status quo. It therefore tends to reflect the political thinking of certain groups of people based on self-serving assumptions and arguments. Admiration of violence as a legitimate means for achieving political objectives is a major component, if not defining characteristic, of such political thinking. In this case, political restrictions and the attitude of ruling governments toward extremist groups are not the reason why the latter advocate violence. Rather, violence in such extremist ideology serves as the solution to what its formulators and proponents perceive as the root causes of all ills of their country, whether social, economic, or political. Racially based political views promoting hatred against ethnic and religious minorities, such as those of the Nazis and white supremacists, belong to this category. There is also another category of political extremism in which extremist measures to achieve political objectives are not its defining characteristic. Rather, it is the "natural" outcome of an environment in which the state is hostile to any type of expression of political views excluding those sanctioned by the state itself; it therefore closes all doors to peaceful expression of popular dissatisfaction with the current situation. The absence of legal avenues for the expression of dissent, on the one hand, and the lack of interest on the part of the ruling elite in addressing popular grievances, on the other, lead to the accumulation of popular dissent. In such a situation, the total exclusion of the people from the political process and the ignoring by the rulers of their demands for change make nonextremist politics and political groups bankrupt and unattractive. Their advocacy of reform and of peaceful means to achieve political objectives seems quite unrealistic at a time when the ruling elite does not allow any meaningful type of political opposition. Under these circumstances, the inability and reluctance of the existing political system to reform itself to meet popular demands make its removal and that of its ruling elite from the political scene a prerequisite for changing the dissatisfactory situation. Hence, radical ideologies became attractive. They offer political violence as the only means for the replacement of the undesirable political system with another one, presumably, but not necessarily, capable of meeting the people's demands. Such extremist or radical ideologies are the ideologies of frustration.

In short, the state's intolerance of any type of political dissent and its reluctance to reform create grounds for the formation of extremist views advocating extremist measures to address the existing problems. The violence used by the state against its opponents makes the use of violence against the state legitimate for disenchanted people and the extremist groups claiming their representation. In such a political environment, political extremism becomes a natural social product created by an authoritarian political system. This is the type of political extremism that has been appearing in the Caucasus and Central Asia.

The overall situation in the three Caucasian and five CA countries has created a suitable environment for the formation of extremist political groups. In these countries, extremism is a response to the worsening overall situation affecting the overwhelming majority of the population. Economic decline, with its lowering of living standards and increase in poverty, has created an atmosphere of anger and dissatisfaction among them. The rampant corruption has further increased popular resentment targeted at the ruling circle. In such a situation, the denial of basic human rights and the suppression of all forms of political activities or any meaningful political opposition have not only increased the popular dissatisfaction, but have eliminated the possibility of a peaceful way for changing the dismal status quo. In the eyes of a growing number of Caucasians and Central Asians, their respective political systems are synonymous with economic ills and abuse of power, incapable of satisfying the needs of their peoples and improving the worsening situation. This environment is ripe for the growth of extremist views advocating a radical objective—that is, the overthrow of the existing political systems by violence, meaning armed struggle. Such an objective will gradually gain popularity among the disenchanted peoples who see no hope for a change for the better as long as the current political systems exist. Consequently, the rise of extremism will be a predictable and "natural" response to the consolidation of authoritarianism at the time of worsening economic situation.

The postindependence era has witnessed the emergence of extremist ideologies and political groups both in the highly unstable Caucasus and in the more stable Central Asia. Hence, the sheer existence of political extremism and groups advocating it are not new phenomena. However, what makes this situation qualitatively different from the rise of extremism during the first few years of independence is a potential for its rapid expansion and deepening. Contrary to expectations at the time of independence, a decade of independence has led to a large and increasing number of people being disillusioned about their governments and their ability to improve the deteriorating situation. It goes without saying that the scenario mentioned will have dire consequences for the affected country itself and also for its respective region as a whole. In consequence, the declining overall situation in the Caucasian and CA countries will further increase their social and political fragility and make them prone to an eruption of extremist views and groups of different sorts. Unless the deteriorating trend is reversed, one should expect the reawakening and rapid expansion of existing extremism that is muted or suppressed in certain countries and the emergence of new extremist pressures in others. Given this likelihood, the rise of extremism will likely push Central Asia and the Caucasus into an unpredictably long period of widespread political tension and uncertainty, with a great potential for escalation into wars in different forms. In turn, this will further worsen the political and security environment in the two regions and have grave negative impact on their economies.

Whereas all the countries of the Caucasus and Central Asia have the potential to give rise to extremism, certain countries are more likely to face active extremism in the near future. The latter are also more prone to its rapid growth. The existence of such countries has created the potential for the expansion of extremist views and activities from one country to others even in the absence of such phenomena in the latter. There is a strong potential for the spillover of extremism from the most vulnerable countries to the least vulnerable ones. The prevailing sentiment of dissatisfaction in all the Caucasian and CA countries and the existence of large minorities with strong ethnic ties with one regional country or another have created this potential. A short analysis of the current situation in both regions should shed light on the argument.

In the Caucasus, the most blatant case is Georgia. This country has been drowning in instability since its independence in 1991. As mentioned earlier, there are two active independence movements in South Ossetia and Abkhazia in full control of their territories. Their war against the government forces ended in 1992 and 1993, respectively, but the subsequent "peace" has been the result of the sheer military weakness of the Georgian government. The two sides have not signed a peace treaty to settle the conflict in a mutually acceptable fashion. Nor is there any realistic hope for such a treaty in the near future. In particular, the Georgian government ruling over a small country cannot possibly accept the independence or reunification of two large parts of its territory with Russia. Reunification with Russia has been the declared intention of the South Ossetian and Abkhaz separatists since 1993. Whether independent or reunified with Russia, the loss of South Ossetia and Abkhazia would lead to the loss of more than half of Georgia's territory, making the rest of the country nonviable. Moreover, this scenario will make the estimated 250,000 to 300,000 internally displaced Georgians from Abkazia permanent refugees in the rest of Georgia. The civil war forced them to leave their homes in Abkhazia to settle in safer areas in the early 1990s. For their part, the governments of the two breakaway regions cannot accept the status quo for long either, as the current situation has been a political and economic limbo for them. They do not enjoy the benefits of membership in Georgia, nor do they have the advantages that might come from full independence. No regional or nonregional state has recognized their independence. Nor is there any indication of this happening in the foreseeable future, despite their de facto independence since 1993. Only their full and official independence or reunification with Russia accepted by the Georgian government can lead to a change in this situation, a move that the Georgian government has no intention of making. All attempts to reach a mutually acceptable settlement through negotiations have so far failed. The failure of UN-sponsored peace talks in New York and a Russian-sponsored meeting between the two sides in Moscow, both in 2000, are but two recent examples.[1]

The fragile peace, which does not serve the long-term interests of either side, may shatter any moment. In fact, the situation has been quite tense since 1993 when the Georgian civil war ended without the roots of the conflict being tackled. The Georgian military or the separatist forces have since violated the ceasefire agreement several times, engaging each other in military confrontations of different magnitude and duration. Recently, many incidents involving violations of the agreement have been reported. The kidnapping of UN peace observers by the Abkhaz separatists in June 2000 was a clear sign of the fragility of the situation.[2] That incident increased the possibility of the resumption of war, a scenario that an increasing number of people on both sides are hoping for. In the same year, skirmishes along the ceasefire line resulted in at least 60 deaths and unspecified numbers of injured people.[3] In early 2001 the situation remained tense, with both sides hinting at a possible resumption of hostilities. In March 2001, five Abkhaz police officials were wounded during a military confrontation between the two sides.[4] Military operations in April and May resulted in 9 deaths and the abduction of 13 people in the Gali district along the ceasefire line; landmine explosions left 5 children dead.[5]

Efforts toward reaching a negotiated settlement of the Abkhaz dispute proved fruitless in the first half of 2001. A new round of negotiation held in March 2001 in Yalta ended with no practical result toward the settlement of the dispute. During the session, the representatives of the Georgian government and the Abkhaz self-declared independent government signed only a ceremonial agreement.[6] The two sides did not go beyond pledges for refraining from violence and for limited cooperation on some cultural and economic issues such as wine-making.[7] There is every indication that the volatile situation is heading toward violence. Unless the situation is changed radically soon, Georgia will be on the road to dismemberment. On the one hand, this is a result of the de facto independence of large parts of the country. On the other, it is a predictable outcome of the gradual process of reintegration of the two breakaway regions into Russia. Russia has supported their independence movements covertly and has treated them differently from its treatment of Georgia. A recent Russian political move makes the latter point clear. In December 2000, the Russian government imposed visa restrictions on Georgians entering Russia but not on the residents of Abkazia and South Ossetia, which neighbor Russia.[8] The move clearly demonstrated the Russian government's policy of their integration into Russia. This seems to be a step toward the future reunification of the two regions with Russia as their inhabitants are now practically treated like Russian citizens.

In addition to the two separatist movements, there is an extremist group formed by the supporters of deceased President Gamsakhurdia. This group does not recognize the authority of the Georgian government, accusing it of ousting the democratically elected president. Since the ousting of President Gamsakhurdia in 1992, the group has tried to overthrow the government by military means. The group has significant military capabilities, and the government's forces have been unable to neutralize it. Operating from its strongholds outside

Tbilisi, over the last decade the group has launched a variety of violent and terrorist activities against the Georgian central government. These activities include the kidnapping of officials, bombings, and major military operations, including temporary occupation of parts of Tbilisi. The most recent operation took place in late 1999 when the group entered the city and reached the proximity of the presidential palace with ease.[9] It has also resorted to political activities leading to violence in most cases. As mentioned before, in May 2001 a demonstration in Tbilisi of about 600 supporters of the deceased president led to a street fight between the police and the demonstrators.[10] The strength and continuity of the group, despite the death of its founder in 1993, demonstrate the growing dissatisfaction of the Georgians with their government and its weakening status. It also indicates the attractiveness of political extremism among the Georgians. The government is clearly unable to control most parts of its country. The economic decline in Georgia will further increase the "popularity" of extremism among the disillusioned Georgians and most probably help the group expand to pose a serious threat to the stability of the Georgian government.

The threat of extremism is not confined in the Caucasus to Georgia, but the rise of such a phenomenon in that country could easily engulf other regional countries. The renewed extremism of active political groups will surely initiate an unpredictably long period of civil war in that country, which will inevitably disrupt its ailing economy. In particular, it will certainly interrupt, if not totally stop, the export of oil from two major Eurasian oil exporters, Azerbaijan and Kazakhstan. These two countries have relied heavily on Georgia for their international exports, a result of the opposition of the American government to the export of their oil via Iran and Russia.[11] By reducing or completely depleting Georgia's revenue from such exports, the further deterioration of its economic situation will increase popular dissatisfaction with the Georgian government. The resulting situation will only serve the interest of extremist groups.

Moreover, any interruption in oil exports via Georgia will worsen the economies of the Caspian region's oil-producers, all of which have experienced major economic difficulties. The opposition of the United States to the use of the Iranian and Russian export routes has forced the American oil companies, which dominate the Eurasian oil industry, to export mainly via Georgia. A pipeline connecting Azerbaijan to Georgia's Black Sea port of Supsa has conducted the bulk of such exports. The exclusive users of the Iranian route have been non-American oil companies, including the state companies of Azerbaijan, Kazakhstan, Turkmenistan, and Uzbekistan, a country with very limited exports. These countries have distributed their portion of exports not connected to any American-dominated oil-development operation via Iran through swap deals. In this case, Iran provides the equivalent amount of oil to the designated buyers at its Persian Gulf oil terminals in return for oil it receives from the Caspian oil exports to be used in its northern refineries. This type of transaction makes sense for Iran, whose oil-fields are located in the southern parts of the country.[12] The Russian route is still used by Azerbaijan to a limited extent and by Kazakhstan to a more significant extent. Their realization of geopolitical realities and also the limitations of the Georgian routes have justified their exports via Russia. Russia has the capability to influence the pace of events in both countries. This is a result of its neighboring status, its economic and military strength, and its strong historical, ethnic, and economic ties with both countries. Consequently, the Russian pipelines connecting Azerbaijan and Kazakhstan to Russia's Black Sea port of Novorossisk have been used since the mid-1990s for the exports of some of the Caspian region's oil exports. However, all its users have significantly decreased their use. The bulk of exports from Azerbaijan, Kazakhstan, Turkmenistan, and Uzbekistan are conducted via Georgia. The closure of the Georgian route for any period of time will therefore have a major impact on their economies. The resulting economic hardship will surely increase popular dissatisfaction, making their peoples more vulnerable to extremist views.

Furthermore, there are concerns about the stability of Georgia in the post-Sheverdnadzhe era. The president is in his seventies, and since he ascended to power in 1993 he has escaped several assassination attempts, the most recent in February 1998.[13] He has managed to contain the forces demanding a war to regain the independent territories, despite the failure of previous attempts. Once he is no longer on the scene, the predictable "war of succession" will likely give more weight to such forces. Their views will be more acceptable for the Georgians, who have seen their country being torn to pieces. Calls for such a policy from among the ruling elite in 2001 indicated the growing frustration of the Georgians with the current stalemate. It is clear to average Georgians that their country will be on the road to dismemberment unless the situation is reversed soon. This reversal is a highly unlikely scenario, if the postindependence history is any indication.

In the Caucasus, Azerbaijan and Armenia are other likely candidates for a rapid emergence of extremism in the form of various radical political ideas or groups. Azerbaijan has suffered from a devastating civil war, resulting in a huge loss of territory and internal displacement of about one million Azeris. The no-war–no-peace situation with Armenia has created a tense situation, which cannot continue indefinitely. The stalemate of the territorial dispute with Armenia and the latter's clear lack of interest in returning the occupied Azeri territory have effectively removed peaceful means for settling the territorial dispute. Certain factors will create a suitable ground for the emergence of radical groups in Azerbaijan, including the frustration of the Azeri refugees with the status quo, the worsening economic situation and its devastating impact on the overwhelming majority of the Azeris, and the inability of the Azeri government to solve the territorial dispute. In such a tense environment, the frustrated population will likely find extremist views proposing a military solution to regain the lost territory more interesting than the wait-and-see policy of their discredited government. Despite President Aliev's rejection of the idea, the growing call in 2001 by the opposition groups, including the Azerbaijan Popular Front, for a war with Armenia indicated the possibility of that scenario.[14] The Azeri government has lost its creditability for a variety of reasons, in particular as a natural outcome of the rampant corruption within the bureaucracy, the government, and the ruling elite of Azerbaijan, as well as the government's growing authoritarianism. In addition to these factors, certain other factors have also further damaged the prestige and the legitimacy of Azerbaijan's political system, while increasing the popularity of any emerging political group demanding a radical end to the current regime. There are endless intra-elite conflicts and sacking of officials by President Aliev, with worsening effects on the overall situation.

As in Georgia, there is also a very strong concern about the future of the country in the post-Aliev era. Most probably, the disappearance of the president from the political scene will lead to a "war of succession" or severe internal conflict. The president's hinted decision that his son, Ilham Aliev, should replace him as president will, if happens, only worsen the situation. Apart from the undemocratic nature of such a decision and the unpopularity of the Aliev family, Ilham Aliev does not have the clout and political experience of his father, who himself has had a hard time running the country.

There are indicators of the growing strength of extremist groups in Armenia. They have posed a serious challenge to the authority of President Kocharian's administration. The Armenian National Movement (ANM), the former ruling party and the major opposition group, is an extremist group with strong right-wing tendencies. The ANM and other extremists, such as the Yerkrapah Union of Karabakh Veterans (YUKV), formed by the Armenians from Nagorno Karabakh, have demanded the resignation of President Kocharian.[15] His government has been under attack by increasingly dissatisfied Armenians. In May 2000, for example, Armenia's capital, Yerevan, witnessed a surge in various antigovernment political activities as well as a series of politically motivated acts of violence. On a number of occasions, including one in June 2001, demonstrators have demanded the resignation of President Kocharian.[16] Intra-elite conflict, described by the president as "the threats to our statehood," has also reached a high point. In 2000, the president dismissed Prime Minister Aram Sarkisian and Defence Minister Vagharshak for their growing dissent.[17] He justified his action as a necessary move "to prevent the escalation of a political threat to the 'foundations of our statehood.'"[18] The extremist right-wing Armenian groups, including the ANM, which has sought to coordinate the activities of all extremist groups, and the YUKV, have been linked to various violent actions. In May 2000, the ex-ANM leader, former Interior Minister Vano Siradeghian, fled Armenia to avoid prosecution for his alleged masterminding of a series of politically related murders.[19] The right-wing extremists were also involved in violent acts against each other. A bodyguard of General Arkady Ter Tadevossian, the leader of a splinter group of the YUKV called the Veterans of the Liberation Struggle, was injured during an armed attack on the general's residence.[20]

The rising threat of extremism has pushed the regional countries toward regional cooperation. The Caucasian and CA countries have become closer to each other and to Russia in their fight against their common threat. On 25 May 2001, the six CIS members of the 1992 CIS Collective Security Treaty (Armenia, Belarus, Kazakhstan, Kyrgyzstan, Russia, and Tajikistan) gathered in Yerevan to create a 3,000-man rapid-reaction force.[21] According to their agreement, the force's headquarters would be in Kyrgyzstan's capital (Bishkek), and each member state would contribute one battalion to the force. The participating countries identified and condemned major sources of concern for their states—namely, terrorism, extremism, organized crime, and drug-trafficking.[22] They affirmed their readiness to repel any further incursion into Central Asia by Islamic militants.[23] Armenia, Kazakhstan, Kyrgyzstan, and Tajikistan have opted for cooperation with Russia despite the fact that such cooperation will strengthen their ties with their former colonial power and increase their dependency on it for their security, a scenario that all have tried to avoid since independence.

When it comes to the threat of extremism, Central Asia has a deceptive profile compared to the Caucasus. Until 1997, when a peace accord ended the Tajik civil war, Tajikistan was the main bedrock for extremism, but the conclusion of the civil war practically ended the era of extremist groups in Tajikistan. The creation of a national reconciliation government comprised of the Tajik elite and the Tajik opposition (both secular and religious groups) turned the entire opposition, including its extremists, into ruling political parties. Extremism has since lost its status as a major political movement, although it has survived in other forms. In fact, a small faction of the Tajik opposition refused to accept the peace accord and remained outside the reconciliation government to continue its political life as an armed opposition. They have since resorted to terrorist activities such as kidnapping and murder of government officials and occasional small-scale military operations. The extremists are very weak numerically and do not enjoy strong popular support. As a part of the government, the Tajik opposition still enjoys the approval of the deprived regions of Tajikistan, where opposition in the form of radical religious and secular groups emerged in the early 1990s. Yet the worsening economic situation in Tajikistan could change the situation quite rapidly. The extremists are small in number and weak militarily, but they still exist. Their radical views and their violent means to achieve their objectives do not currently appeal to the majority of the Tajiks, whose poor country has been exhausted by a five-year civil war. However, their frustration with the persistence of economic and social problems could easily change this situation and make them interested in the politics of extremists. A recent incident showed the fragility of the situation in Tajikistan and the capability of the extremists to challenge the authority of the Tajik government. In June 2001, Rahmon Sanginov, a former field commander of the Tajik opposition forces opposed to the peace accord, took hostage several police officers and civilians.[24] Concerned about the backlash of a military approach to the event, the government ruled out resort to force and secured their release through negotiations.

Apart from Tajikistan, Central Asia contains sources of extremism with the potential of rapid expansion. The most dangerous case is the Ferghana Valley. As mentioned earlier, the valley hosts two major sources of threat. The first is the growing international drug-trafficking. The drug-traffickers have had military confrontations with the combined forces of Kyrgyzstan, Tajikistan, and Uzbekistan. So far, this has been the most important source of instability and threat to the security of the three states sharing the valley. Their poor economy, resulting in unemployment and poverty, will ensure the growth of the drug "industry" and related illegal activities such as trafficking in arms. Drug-related activities are becoming a major source of employment and income in the valley and elsewhere in all the CIS countries. The second source of concern for the three CA countries sharing the Ferghana Valley is the rise of armed political opposition in the valley. The armed religious extremist group called the Islamic Movement of Uzbekistan (IMZ) is still too weak to pose a serious threat to the stability of those countries, although they all have legitimate concerns about its threat. The IMZ has conducted its terrorist activities throughout the entire valley. It allegedly seeks to establish a united Islamic state in the valley or to overthrow its three governments, according to different sources. The government of Uzbekistan has been especially concerned as the IMZ has focused mainly on Uzbekistan. Its major military operation was reportedly conducted in the summer of 2000, when the regional military forces were engaged in a large-scale war with various armed groups in the valley which lasted until the following winter.[25] The incident resulted in unspecified large numbers of casualties especially in Kyrgyzstan and Uzbekistan. The Uzbek government claims that the IMZ was the main force fighting its troops and those of other regional countries, but there is little evidence to sub-stantiate that claim.[26] Given the history of wide-scale military opera-tion in the Ferghana Valley and the strength of drug-traffickers, there is little doubt that the latter formed the bulk of the attacking forces. Their purpose was to secure a safe passage to Kazakhstan via Uzbek-istan from where they export drugs to Russia and Europe.[27] Yet it is certain that the IMZ was also involved in the fighting for its own objectives. Regardless of the real extent of the involvement of the IMZ, the Uzbek government has since arrested large numbers of people on charges of involvement in the event. In a recent case, in June 2001 four courts in Tashkent sentenced 73 ethnic Tajik citizens of Uzbekistan to prison sentences ranging from 3 to 18 years for their alleged support of the IMZ fighters during their summer 2000 fighting with the Uzbek forces.[28]

The extremist groups do not yet pose an immediate threat to the CA countries, but there is no doubt that they are heading that way, should the situation not improve. All these countries are vulnerable to such a threat, as many factors have created a situation conducive to a rapid expansion of extremist views. The declining economic situation has frustrated the Central Asians with the state of affairs to the extent that most of them could be quite receptive to extremist views and political activities. The social fragility of the CA countries makes the spillover of radical antigovernment sentiments from one country to another a feasible scenario. However, the source of spillover is not limited to these countries. Despite the fall of the Taliban and the creation of an interim government in Afghanistan, the continuation of instability and low-level fighting among rival Afghan groups, which could escalate into a civil war engulfing the entire country, have created a strong potential for the expansion of instability and war from Afghanistan into neighboring CA countries.

The fear that Central Asia might drown in a long period of instabil-ity, through either internal or external factors, has resulted in the formation of the Shanghai Cooperation Organisation (SCO). The SCO consists of Kazakhstan, Kyrgyzstan, Tajikistan, China, and Russia. Also known as the Shanghai Five, the SCO was formed in 1996 mainly to settle border disputes between China and the four CIS countries (Russia, Kazakhstan, Kyrgyzstan and Tajikistan) sharing borders with it. It has since gradually developed into a vehicle for their collective efforts to combat terrorism and extremism, as they all have strong reasons for concern about these phenomena. Russia and China have become increasingly worried about the expansion of militant groups in Chechnya and Xinjiang, respectively. Fear of disintegration has aligned them with their CA neighbors, which have their own reasons for concern. In particular, over two decades of civil war in Afghanistan have made them all especially worried about the impact of the instability in that country on the growth of extremism in their countries. Their most recent meeting was held in June 2001 in the city of Shanghai, the same location as their first meeting in 1996.[29] Although the details of the decisions regarding their cooperation have yet to be released, it is known that the participants were particularly concerned about the threat of extremism from Afghanistan. During their meeting, the five member states signed an agreement to fight terrorism and extremism.[30] The CA countries agreed to help China and Russia deal with what they perceive as "an organized extremist threat" in return for receiving support from the two powers in their fighting with their own extremists.[31] This threat and the growing concern of Uzbekistan about the worsening situation in the Ferghana Valley motivated that country to join the SCO during its June meeting.[32] Regional cooperation has not, of course, been limited to the SCO. As mentioned earlier, the members of the CIS Collective Security Treaty (Armenia, Belarus, Kazakhstan, Kyrgyzstan, Russia, and Tajikistan) agreed in their Yerevan meeting of 2001 to form a rapid-reaction force to fight terrorists and extremists as well. The two-regional cooperation groups demonstrate the growing concern among the Caucasian and CA countries about the emerging threat of extremism.

NATIONALISM AS A COUNTERMEASURE FOR THE ELITES

There is no doubt that the probable rise of radical political groups will pose a serious challenge to the stability of the Caucasian and Central Asian states. The worsening situation will surely increase the depth of the threat of such a phenomenon and make it harder for these states to deal with the challenge. In the absence of material resources to eliminate the economic and social roots of this destructive phenomenon, the ruling elite will have to resort to the available "resources" to prevent the expansion of extremist groups and/or to seek their uprooting. Historically, promoting nationalism in various forms, including the extreme (e.g., chauvinism), has been the most frequently used measure by rulers once they face the threat of expanding hostile ideologies. When popular dissatisfaction with the state of affairs is high and growing, a way to divert the people's attention from the roots of their dissatisfaction is to stimulate and manipulate their nationalist sentiments. Such sentiments therefore help the elite "hide" its inability to address the major economic and social problems that unsettle its people.

Nationalism strengthens the power of rulers in a variety of ways. It helps them improve their image and uplift their popularity by elevating them to the status of defender of their people's national heritage. Because of its radical appearance, nationalism is an attractive ideology to the population at large. In particular, it is fascinating for young people, who form the social strata most vulnerable to extremist ideologies. Nationalism can therefore assist the ruling elite to secure the loyalty or at least the positive attitude of the youth toward the establishment in various attractive forms through political groups and movements. As a result, nationalism weakens the opposition ideologies, whether moderate or extremist, by lowering their attractiveness and denying them large numbers of recruits from among the dissatisfied people. Their would-be members are likely to find the government-sponsored ideology based on nationalist sentiments more appealing and "natural" than those of the under-suppression opposition, at least for a while. Nationalism also helps the ruling elite to continue to expand its suppression of the opposition, including extremists, under the nationalist pretext. This is a more convincing excuse than others for the average person. Suppressing opposition under the widely used charge of it weakening the government or defaming leaders, for example, can hardly secure the approval of the general population. They are too dissatisfied with their political systems to accept such charges. The incompetence and corruption within the ruling elite and their bureaucratic and security apparatus will make such charges meaningless and unacceptable for the people. On the other hand, suppression of the opposition is much easier and more acceptable if the opposition groups are portrayed as acting against national interests, advocating foreign ideologies, and carrying out the will of hostile foreign countries.

Nationalism is a means for the ruling elites of the Caucasian and CA countries to address their well-founded concerns about their long-term stability. This ideology can at a time of trouble contribute to the creation of a national consensus by which the elites can consolidate their power basis. It has become an increasingly important component of statecraft in these eight countries since their independence in 1991. Nationalism is not a new phenomenon for them. To a limited extent, it emerged during the last few years of the Soviet Union when all 15 Soviet republics were experiencing the upsurge of nationalist sentiments in various forms. The growing popular dissatisfaction among the Soviet people and the weakening of Soviet ties among the republics provided grounds for the rise of long-suppressed nationalist aspirations among the different peoples of the Soviet Union, a multi-ethnic empire dominated by the Russians. Whereas nationalism was flourishing in many parts of the Soviet Union such as the Ukraine and the Baltic republics (Estonia, Latvia, and Lithuania), it was a very weak political force in the Caucasian and CA republics and of little practical significance to the pace of events. Of course, there were differences among these republics in a comparative sense. In general, nationalist movements attacking the Soviet political system and the predominance of the Russians in all aspects of life were not very strong and were almost nonexistent in Central Asia, but they were more significant in the Caucasus. In that region, nationalism emerged not as a challenging force to the Soviet system, but as a form of rivalry between the Azeris and Armenians, manifested in the bloody confrontation between the two neighbors over Nagorno Karabakh. In comparison to other Caucasian countries, nationalism was stronger in Georgia, but it was not as extensive and intensive as it was in the Baltic republics, for instance. The lack of nationalism as a strong political force in the Caucasus and Central Asia was evident in the absence of enthusiasm among their peoples for independence and the creation of independent states, a reflection of their extensive reliance on the Soviet central government.

Nationalism emerged as a main political force in the post-Soviet era. The fall of the Soviet Union imposed independence on the eight Caucasian and CA republics at a time when they were unprepared for it. Two factors contributed to its rise in the postindependence era. On the one hand, the termination of Moscow's generous assistance to these newly independent countries suddenly severed their tie of dependence on Moscow. On the other, the ex-Soviet elites ruling these republics had to resort to an alternative ideology to break with the now undesirable past and to legitimize their rule in the postindependence period. They needed to create a consensus within their respective republics to help them pass through the agonizing period of transition from the crumbling Soviet economic and social systems to a hoped-for free-enterprise economy with its corresponding social system. Thus, nationalism emerged as a result of a sudden and unplanned political development, which forced them all to rely on their own resources and therefore rediscover themselves as nations different from the Russians. As a byproduct of the erupting nationalism, the Russians who had ruled over their territories for about two centuries now seemed more than ever like colonizers. Independence gave them the chance to reanalyze the Russians as the invaders who conquered their territories and forced them to accept their rule and culture. The process of dealing with the colonial past and the rediscovery of their own heritage helped awaken the hidden and suppressed nationalism. Thus, nationalism appeared on the political scene as a cultural revival in the postindependence era. There was a sudden and growing interest in their pre-Russian/Soviet era and a desire to restore their suppressed culture, including their languages and art. This process has continued to this date.

Nationalism as a popular movement for the revival of cultural and historical heritage has been a predictable outcome of independence in the Caucasian and CA countries. This phenomenon has created a natural setting for the expansion of a radical type of nationalism being promoted by the ruling elites toward certain political ends. Different versions of extreme forms of nationalism have been adopted, such as hegemonism and chauvinism. In the Caucasus, the rise of nationalism has almost exclusively centred on radical, extremist, and chauvinistic forms. The eruption of Georgian nationalism with strong anti-minority components has been credited with contributing to the civil war in Georgia in the early 1990s. The Georgian government under both President Gamsakhurdia and President Sheverdnadzhe has provoked sentiments against the South Ossetians and the Abkaz. In particular, the extremist politics of Gamsakhurdia was a major factor leading to their independence wars.[33] Needless to say, the people of South Ossetia and Abkhaz had several reasons for their rebellion against the Georgian government. However, the latter's intolerance of all their demands dated back to the Soviet era, and its resort to an iron-fist policy toward those regions ensured the radicalization of their independence movements. The South Ossetians and the Abkhaz adopted military means following the military response of the Georgian government to their demands. Hence, the emergence of Georgian nationalism in its chauvinistic form, intolerant of any ethnic demand, provoked the radicalization of South Ossetian and Abkhaz nationalism. Besides the efforts of Russia to manipulate the Georgian independence movements to achieve its own short- and long-term objectives, this policy has contributed to the creation of the fragile no-war–no-peace situation since the end of civil war in 1993.

Likewise, nationalism has emerged in Azerbaijan and Armenia in an extremist form. Late in the 1980s when both countries were still Soviet republics, nationalism emerged in Armenia as a demand for the reunification of Nagorno Karabakh with Armenia.[34] In this case, Armenian nationalism promoted by its ruling elite took a radical expansionist form sanctioning the modification of the Armenian–Azeri borders by military force. Not surprisingly, this led to a war with Azerbaijan, as a large part of its territory was about to be separated from it by force. Azeri nationalism emerged in response to Armenian expansionist nationalism within the context of a war to defend the Azeri territorial integrity. It therefore took a radical and military form led by the Azeri political elite. The two sides became engaged in a bloody war, resulting in tens of thousands of deaths and large numbers of internally displaced refugees, which further increased ethnic hatred in their respective countries. Thus, nationalism in Armenia and Azerbaijan has developed from ethnic hatred and surfaced in a violent/military form. The war ended in 1994, but the territorial conflict still remains. The situation has radicalized both sides and provoked in both countries the emergence of extremist views demanding a military situation to end the current stalemate.

In Central Asia, nationalism has also emerged in radical forms, although in a much smaller scale compared to the Caucasus. The government of Uzbekistan has promoted Uzbek nationalism from the very beginning of independence, accompanied by strong hegemonic tendencies.[35] Uzbekistan has sought to establish itself as the regional power in Central Asia, an aim toward which some of its characteristics have contributed. As it is relatively industrialized, the country has the largest population and the strongest military force in that region. It shares borders with all CA countries because it is located in the center of the region. These characteristics have offered the means and opportunities to the Uzbeks to aspire to determine the pace of events in their region. Historical factors have also strengthened this aspiration. The existence of certain cities serves as a reminder of a glorious past, which could be revived given their relatively strong status. Samarkand was the capital of the Mongol Empire for a long time. Tashkent, Bukhara, and Khiva were the capitals of the three strong CA *khantaes* [states] ruling over the region or large parts of it before their annexation by Russia.

The rise of Uzbek nationalism has been a source of concern for the Tajiks, whose smaller and significantly poorer country shares a long border with Uzbekistan. The Uzbeks have territorial claim to the Uzbek-dominated part of Tajikistan located in the Ferghana Valley, including the city of Khojand. The region has shown signs of a desire to unify with Uzbekistan. In the wake of the 1997 peace accord, the political leaders of the region who receive assistance from the Uzbek government were against the peace accord. Being opposed to the creation of a coalition government, including the opposition Islamic groups, they threatened to secede from Tajikistan to unify with Uzbekistan. When the Islamic–Democratic coalition took power in 1992, these Khojandi leaders also threatened to secede in the event of the creation of an Islamic state by the coalition.[36] They have since been implicated in coup attempts and violent military activities against the Tajik government. The Tajiks view them with suspicion for their efforts to break up Tajikistan and to impose a new round of civil war on them. The Tajiks are also concerned about the Uzbek government's direct threat to their security, as it has sought to influence the internal politics of Tajikistan. The government has been accused of masterminding at least one abortive coup attempt in late 1999 through the Khojandi leaders.[37] Given this situation, the Tajiks have strong reasons for their concern about Uzbek nationalism, which has created anxiety and fear about their territorial integrity and independence.

Uzbek nationalism has also been a source of concern for other regional countries, mainly Kazakhstan and Kyrgyzstan. The Uzbeks have territorial claims to both countries. The vague and unmarked borders between Soviet republics, which had not been seen as an issue given their membership in the same country, opened doors to territorial and border conflicts in the preindependence era. In many cases, the borders were drawn without regard to historical facts and the ethnic composition of cities and villages. As a result, the Uzbeks do not recognize the Soviet border(s) between their country and Kazakhstan and Kyrgyzstan, which in some cases leave many Uzbeks in those countries. Since independence, the Uzbek government has been involved in a border dispute with Kazakhstan and Kyrgyzstan over areas inside the latter countries, including those where the inhabitants are mainly ethnic Uzbeks. The dispute has worsened over the last two years, as Uzbekistan has used force to change the borderline in certain regions on several occasions. As a recent example, in 1999 Dooronbek Sadyrbayev, a member of the Kyrgyz parliament, stated that "the Uzbek officials [were] shifting the border between the two countries in Uzbekistan's favor."[38] Another recent example took place in 2000 when Uzbek troops penetrated into Kazakh territory and changed the borderline by force. This type of behavior has been a source of concern for Kazakhstan and Kyrgyzstan, which are militarily much weaker than Uzbekistan. Uzbekistan's nationalistic claim has worsened Kazakh–Uzbek ties, which have already been damaged by many other issues such as their major disagreements on how to deal with the environmental disaster of the Aral Sea, a dying lake between Kazakhstan and Uzbekistan.[39]

In the case of Kyrgyzstan, besides border disputes, Uzbekistan has had a territorial claim to the Osh region of Kyrgyzstan for a long time.[40] This mainly Uzbek-dominated region became the scene of an armed and bloody ethnic conflict between its Uzbek and Kyrgyz inhabitants in 1990, a year prior to the fall of the Soviet Union.[41] The conflict had the potential to escalate into a war between Kyrgyzstan and Uzbekistan as armed Uzbeks from the neighboring Andijan region in Uzbekistan unsuccessfully tried to cross the border into Kyrgyzstan to help their kin.[42] The policy of restraint of the then two Soviet republics prevented that scenario at that time. Nonetheless, there is no guarantee that in any similar situation in the future the governments of Uzbekistan and Kyrgyzstan will find enough convincing reasons to do the same. The worsening economic situation in Kyrgyzstan and the growing Kyrgyz nationalism with its clear policy of preference for ethnic Kyrgyz in the job market will likely contribute to a fresh rise of ethnic strife. Such phenomenon will be a likely scenario for dragging the Uzbek and Kyrgyz governments into a conflict. These governments have not been on good terms with each other, because of various trade disputes regarding especially the sale of Kyrgyz water to Uzbekistan and of Uzbek natural gas to Kyrgyzstan. In particular, disagreements over the pricing of Uzbek natural gas and the inability of the Kyrgyz government to pay for the imported gas have resulted in frequent annual cuts of Uzbek exported gas to Kyrgyzstan. Added to the trade disputes, the Uzbek government has criticized the Kyrgyz government since the late 1990s for its "lack of cooperation" with Uzbekistan in its fight against armed groups in the Ferghana Valley.[43] This criticism comes notwithstanding the fierce fighting in 2000 of Kyrgyz troops with the armed groups in its Betkhen region, which falls within its share of the valley. The existence of several sources of conflict in the relations between Kyrgyzstan and Uzbekistan has created grounds for the growth of anti-Kyrgyz sentiment in Uzbekistan, and this will help foster Uzbek nationalism.

FEASIBLE SCENARIOS FOR THE FUTURE: CIVIL WARS, INTERSTATE WARS, AND REGIONAL WARS

History has demonstrated that the rise of nationalism in a country is in itself neither positive nor negative. What determines its impact on the affected countries is the overall political, economic, and social context within which it develops. This context determines its form and objectives, and therefore its positive or negative implications for the affected countries and their regions. Following this historical fact, the rise of nationalism in the Caucasian and CA countries has been a very negative phenomenon. Given the various sources of political and ethnic discontent, its emergence has not strengthened these newly independent states. On the contrary, the rise of nationalism in all these countries has contributed to their instability and weakened their social fabric by awakening ethnic rivalry and independence movements. The result has been civil wars, which have been intensive and quite destructive, especially in the Caucasus. It is true that currently there is no active civil war in these two regions, but the absence of such wars—and, in general, major active destabilizing forces—should not be mistaken for peace. For the reasons discussed earlier, there is ground for the rise of instability in different forms and intensity in both regions. Whereas all countries have a suitable situation for instability, even those which currently seem stable (e.g., Turkmenistan) will not be immune to instability. On the one hand, the highly personalized regime of Turkmenistan—which derives its legitimacy from the prestige, charisma, and cult of personality of its leader (President Safarmorad Niyazov)—is likely to fall apart when he is out of the political scene. In such a case, all suppressed grievances with the political system and with its top officials, as well as other suppressed issues such as ethnic conflicts, will suddenly erupt. On the other hand, the ethnic makeup of the Caucasus and Central Asia and, in particular, the existence of large regional ethnic groups in every single country, especially in Central Asia, will guarantee the expansion of instability from those countries more prone to instability into the others.

Civil wars are the most likely forms of instability in both the Caucasus and Central Asia, but evidence suggests that instability will not be confined to civil wars. Should civil wars begin for whatever reason, certain factors will create a potential for their escalation to interstate and regional wars. Needless to say, such a scenario will be devastating for each region and its member states, all of which require a long period of peace as a prerequisite for their economic development. Yet the threat of escalation will not be confined to the possibilities mentioned, as the existence of certain regional—Iran, China, Turkey, and Russia—and nonregional—United States—powers with long-term interests in the two regions has created a potential for their involvement in any regional military conflict.

The four regional powers have long-term political and economic interests in the Caucasus and Central Asia, which neighbor their countries. To different extents, they all have ethnic, cultural, religious, historical, and economic ties with them or one of them with which they share a border. These ties facilitate their penetration into the regions or parts of them, depending on the case.[44] Those regions in need of extensive development projects offer a potentially lucrative market to the four countries, while their oil and natural-gas resources offer opportunities of a different nature and extent to all of them. Gaining influence in the countries of Central Asia and the Caucasus will also serve their political interests. It will also uplift or consolidate their regional and international status. Furthermore, they are interested in the political stability of these regions as their instability could destabilize their countries to a varying extent, given their vicinity and/ or various ties with the regions. In search of influence, Iran, China, Turkey, and Russia are worried about the domination of each other over the two regions, which could turn the regions into unfriendly or hostile neighbors for others. Finally, these regional powers, with the exception of Turkey, are worried about the presence of a nonregional power—the United States—in Central Asia and the Caucasus. This is partly because of security concerns about its presence in their vicinity, as they all have reasons for suspicion about its long-term objectives. It is also partly because of their unhappiness about U.S. efforts to domi-nate the potentially lucrative oil industry of the Caspian region. In particular, Iran and Russia are angry at its efforts to exclude them from any involvement in the Caspian oil industry, including oil exports via their countries.[45] For the reasons mentioned, Iran, China, and Russia have sought to prevent the growth of an American presence in the Caucasus and Central Asia, with which they have long borders.

The United States has a twofold interest in these regions. Although their energy resources are not a substitute for those of the Persian Gulf, the significant oil and, to a lesser extent, natural-gas reserves are of importance to America as it has sought to diversify its energy suppliers.[46] Apart from economic interests, the Americans have a political and strategic objective in these regions—that is, preventing Iran and Russia from gaining influence there.

Because of their interests in and/or links to the Caucasus and Cen-tral Asia, it is quite feasible that the five powers may be dragged into any future military conflict in those regions. This could come about through their intentional or unintentional engagement in interstate or regional wars instigated for one reason or another. In the event of such a scenario, the destructive nature of instability in the Caucasus and Central Asia will spread far beyond the regions themselves as the escalation of any military conflict could destabilize large parts of Asia and Europe.

The escalation of domestic conflicts to major military confronta-tions is a very feasible scenario given the postindependence history of the two regions and their various potentials. The Caucasus serves as a very clear example. The Azeri-Armenian conflict, which began as an ethnic/territorial dispute within the Soviet Union, rapidly turned into a major conflict despite the efforts of the Soviet leaders to defuse the tense situation. The dispute developed into a bloody civil war in Azerbaijan as the Armenian population of Nagorno Karabakh resorted to arms to secure their independence from Azerbaijan and unify with Armenia. The direct and extensive military assistance of Armenia to the Karabakhi Armenian militants turned the civil war into an inter-state war between Armenia and Azerbaijan which lasted for about six years. After the fall of the Soviet Union in 1991, the Azeri-Armenian war involved certain regional countries on the side of one or the other, a pattern still in place to date.

When the Caucasian republics became independent, no regional power was in favor of the separation of Nagorno Karabakh and its unification with Armenia. Besides other factors, separation of territories by force could have set a precedent for their own countries. The existence of active separatist and independence movements in Russia (Chechnya) and Turkey (Kurdish region) made them worried about such a scenario. Added to the threat of pan-Turkism with its design on Iranian Azerbaijan, Iran's eight years of devastating war with Iraq (which sought to annex the Iranian Province of Khuzestan) made Iran an active opponent of geographical change by military force. However, certain factors pushed Russia and Iran to take sides with Armenia and assist it to different extents, although neither country approved of Armenia's territorial ambition. Russia's assistance to Armenia was mainly in the form of supplying arms, but that of Iran was mainly of a nonmilitary nature, including the supply of medical goods and services. The major factor behind these two countries' assistance to Armenia was the anti-Iranian and anti-Russian policy of Azeri President Abulfazel Elchibey.[47] Another was the rise of pan-Turkism in Azerbaijan as a result of his ascension to presidency. His extremist and expansionist view of creating Greater Azerbaijan at the territorial expense of Iran and Russia was a direct threat to those countries. Yet another factor was the growing influence of Turkey in Azerbaijan. The Elchibey era opened doors to a rapid growth of his main regional supporter—pro-American and NATO-member Turkey. This became a reason for security concern for both Iran and Russia. Using its ethnic and/or historical ties with the Turkic Central Asians and the Azeris, Turkey was initially advancing in almost all the southern CIS countries, all of which were in a very desperate situation during the first few years of independence.[48] This advancement was alarming, given Turkey's regional ambitions. The latter were reflected in its overt policy of turning itself into the regional power in West Asia, which motivated it in 1992 to aim to establish—but without success—a Turkey-dominated federation of all the Turkic states of Central Asia and the Caucasus.[49] Added to this, Turkey's mostly indirect promotion of pan-Turkism was a clear security threat to both Iran and Russia. Its objective of creating Greater Turkey or Greater Turan—a state comprising all Turkic and Turkic-speaking ethnic groups between China and the Mediterranean Sea—would lead to the separation of parts of their countries falling within that plan. Finally, the growing influence of the West—in particular, the United States—in the Caucasus was a major source of concern for Iran and Russia. This was partly a result of Turkey's increasing influence in Azerbaijan and, to a lesser extent, in Georgia. It was also partly because of the direct growing presence of different Western countries, and mainly the United States, as a result of the domination of the Caspian oil industry by their oil companies.

The fall of the Elchibey regime in 1993 changed the situation to some extent. Azerbaijan's humiliating defeat in its war with Armenia and the rampant corruption of the Elchibey administration led to a sharp decline in the popularity of pan-Turkism in that country and removed its immediate threat from the regional political scene. The more balanced foreign policy of the Aliev regime helped improve ties between Azerbaijan and its two large neighbors, Iran and Russia. However, the pro-American tendencies of the new regime and its continued antipathy toward Iran and Russia, although in different forms and to a lesser extent, did not change the overall situation drastically.

The Aliev era has had an impact on the attitude of Iran and Russia toward the Azeri-Armenian conflict. Russia has not changed its pro-Armenian policy toward the conflict, although its economic ties with Azerbaijan have increased. Its military alliance with Armenia is not a secret, nor is the existence of various Russian military facilities in that country. Russia has been the main arms supplier to Armenia. However, Iran's relations with Azerbaijan have expanded and improved dramatically.[50] Having friendly ties with Armenia, better ties with Azerbaijan have motivated Iran to pursue a neutral position toward Armenia and Azerbaijan and function also on occasions as a mediator between them for a peaceful settlement of conflicts. Yet the unstable political nature of the Iranian relations with Azerbaijan as a result of that country's on-and-off hostile approach to Iran has kept these relations significantly less friendly than those with Armenia. Iran has every interest in the stability of the Caucasus and in particular peace along its northern borders with Armenia and Azerbaijan. For this reason, it has no interest in the resumption of the Azeri-Armenian war.

Yet, the status of Iran's relations with Azerbaijan could convince Iran of the merits of changing its policy of neutrality in the Azeri-

Armenian conflict, a policy that it has pursued since the early 1990s. There are at least two scenarios under which Iran could find incentives to support Armenia should the war be resumed. The deterioration of the current peaceful but unpredictable relations between Iran and Azerbaijan is one conceivable scenario. In particular, efforts by Azerbaijan or the United States to exclude Iran totally from Azerbaijan to deny it political and economic gains will certainly create strong motivations for Iran. Azerbaijan's future closer military ties with NATO or the United States, with a clear security implication for Iran, will be another major incentive for that country. Iran's expression of deep concern about Azerbaijan's receipt of two American military boats in early 2001 demonstrated its extreme sensitivity to Azeri-American military ties.[51]

Russia, on its part, will have strong reasons to side with Armenia in any future Azeri-Armenian war. Azerbaijan's growing relations with the United States and its efforts to seek NATO's protection or membership will not leave too many strong reasons for Russia to become neutral. Added to this, like Iran, Russia has been angry at America's policy of bypassing its route for the export of Caspian oil and natural gas, including that from Azerbaijan, aimed at denying it economic and political gains.

Turkey has also been involved in the Azeri-Armenian conflict. Its involvement began after the fall of the Soviet Union and the independence of the two Caucasian republics drowned in a bloody conflict. Promoting itself as the "big brother" of all Turkic and Turkic-speaking peoples, Turkey's interest in finding a foothold in the neighboring Caucasus aligned it with Azerbaijan. Historical conflicts with and hostility toward Armenia and its fear about the rising Armenian nationalism were its other strong incentives. The Armenians have territorial claims to eastern parts of Turkey, which could reemerge as an active nationalist demand, a nightmare for Turkey which has suffered for years from an armed Kurdish separatist movement in the same area. Apart from political, security, and historical factors, economic factors have played a major role, if not the major one, in this taking of sides. Turkey's heavy reliance on imported oil made it especially interested in Azerbaijan's oil resources. Equally important, Turkey wanted to establish itself as the main export route for Azerbaijan's oil resources, with obvious economic gains and political importance for the Turks. Turkey's taking sides with Azerbaijan did not help the

Azeris in their war with Armenia. Turkey's negligible financial resources and limited indigenous military production made it too weak an ally for Azerbaijan to have a major impact on the pace of war. The latter's acceptance of a humiliating ceasefire at a time when about one-fifth of its territory was under Armenian occupation also humiliated Turkey and weakened its influence in Azerbaijan. For the various reasons mentioned, it has since remained on the side of Azerbaijan.

The history of Turkey's ties with Azerbaijan and Armenia since 1991 suggests that Turkey will have every reason to support Azerbaijan in its future wars with Armenia. This will be regardless of its significance for the victory of the Azeris. In particular, Turkey's bid to make itself the main oil export route for Azerbaijan, reflected in its proposed Baku–Ceyhan pipeline, will force it to take sides with that country. That, at least, will be a necessity to ensure the stability of Azerbaijan, an absolute prerequisite for constructing any pipeline in that country.[52] In such a case, Turkey's contribution to Azerbaijan's military efforts may well worsen the situation by prolonging the war and making it ripe for escalation. Among other considerations, Iran and Russia will find it difficult to remain indifferent to Turkey's military involvement in a war along their borders. Such involvement will most probably provoke their engagement in the war as well. The extension of Turkey's involvement and its impact on the pace of war will be a major factor determining the extent of the Iranian and Russian involvement.

Georgia serves as another example of how a civil war may escalate. Separatist movements emerged in Abkhazia and South Ossetia almost immediately after its independence. The roots of the movements lay in ethnic conflicts between their ethnically distinct peoples and the Georgians. However, they grew strength as a result of two factors: the harsh policy of the Georgian government to the regions' emerging ethnic movements and Russia's growing interest in them. The Russians have found many reasons for their interest in these movements. For one, Russia has viewed them as an opportunity for the reestablishment of its influence in the Caucasus in general, and in Georgia in particular. The inability of the Georgian government to restore its sovereignty over the two regions by military force made it accept a ceasefire with South Ossetia in 1992 and another with Abkhazia in 1993, leaving large parts of its country out of its control. Without a doubt, this development has made the Georgian government very weak and vulnerable to foreign pressure, especially that of Russia. Whether the Georgians like it or not, Russia has become the key to any future settlement between the Georgian government and the separatist movements. Russia has used this leverage to prevent Georgia's total shift toward the Western countries and particularly the United States; this shift has been a major security concern for Russia, which already felt threatened because of the eastward expansion of NATO.

Russia's support of the two movements has also had a security dimension. The two rebellious regions share borders with the troubled Caucasian region of Russia, including Chechnya. It is no wonder that the Russian government has wanted to ensure they have a cooperative and friendly attitude toward Russia. This attitude has enabled it to cut the Chechen militants' supply route from Georgia. Russia has had a major reason for its involvement in the Georgian civil conflict: As a result of the fall of the Soviet Union, most Soviet Black Sea ports are in non-Russian republics, and it therefore needs to expand its limited access to the Black Sea. Abkhazia's coastline with the Black Sea and its port of Sukhumi can address the Russian access problem.

For those matters and also for ensuring the security of their southern borders, the Russians seem to have initiated the gradual process of reunification of the two Georgian regions with their country. Apart from the direct military and nonmilitary assistance that these regions receive from Russia, the December 2000 visa imposition on Georgia reflected the Russians' reunification plan.[53] The Russian visa policy effectively treated the inhabitants of Abkhazia and South Ossetia as Russian nationals by excluding them from the policy. Direct and friendly ties of different Russian political and administrative organs with those of the two Georgian regions have been other indicators of the reunification plan. For example, in early 2001 the Russian parliament sent a congratulatory message to the parliament of Abkhazia on its tenth anniversary, a body unlawful under the Georgian constitution. The Russian message gave recognition to the parliament as separate from that of Georgia, a move unmatched by any other country. It also implied Russia's disregard of the Georgian government's efforts to regain control over the breakaway region.

Finally, Russia has had a clear economic reason for its support of the Georgian separatist movements. Their weakening of the authority and power of the Georgian government and creation of uncertainty about the stability of Georgia have raised doubts about the wisdom of exporting Caspian oil via that country.[54] Given the American government's absolute opposition to the use of Iran as an export route, the security uncertainty in Georgia leaves Russia as the only remaining export option. For all the reasons mentioned, it will come as little surprise if Russia actively supports the two regions in any future war against the Georgian forces.

As in the Caucasus, political dissent in any single country of Central Asia could develop into a major destabilizing event leading to a military conflict with a strong potential for external expansion. As mentioned earlier, the Tajik civil war serves as a very clear example of the fragility of the situation in that region. A political conflict between the old and new political guards escalated to a five-year-long full-fledged civil war. Many factors both forced and motivated all regional countries, excluding Turkmenistan, to engage themselves in the civil war on the side of the Tajik government. For the CA elites, all of whom were unpopular Soviet regional bosses, the efforts of new political groups unrelated to the old Soviet elite to replace the latter in Tajikistan was a bad precedent. The existence of political dissent to a varying degree and numerous economic problems in the CA countries made them all fearful of the duplication of the same scenario in their own countries. Furthermore, the ethnic composition of the region made the expansion of the war in Tajikistan to its neighbors, Uzbekistan and Kyrgyzstan, a very realistic possibility. Uzbeks and Tajiks live in large communities in all three countries. They also live in Kazakhstan and Turkmenistan in smaller, but still numerically significant, communities. No wonder if all of them provided assistance, including military supplies, to the Tajik governments to contain the civil war. [55] Yet Uzbekistan became extensively involved in the conflict and became the major arms suppliers to the government forces, while using its own military force to assist the seemingly weak Tajik government.[56] A major reason, among several others, for Uzbekistan's extensive involvement was that it was the most vulnerable regional country to the Tajik civil war, because of two demographic facts—namely, Uzbekistan's having the largest Tajik minority group in the region, and Tajikistan's having the largest regional Uzbek minority community. This demographic peculiarity has created a strong ethnic tie between the two countries, making these neighbors very vulnerable to instability in each other's country.

The civil war in Tajikistan showed how a domestic conflict could easily escalate into a civil war. It also demonstrated the strong potential for regional countries being dragged in. However, a number of factors prevented the expansion of the war to other regional countries in the 1990s. The stalemate in the civil war was a major factor, as neither the Tajik opposition nor the Tajik government could eliminate the other. The devastation of Tajikistan's economy was another, as it meant that the continuation of the war would be national suicide. Cooperation among the regional countries and their two neighbors (Iran and Russia) was yet another fact. The latter made peace negotiations and the conclusion of the 1997 peace accord feasible.

However, the situation in the first decade of the twenty-first century is very different from that of the last decade. All the regional countries are more fragile, thanks to their economic decline and growing popular dissent. Under the new circumstances, the resumption of the Tajik civil war, which is a possibility, could easily expand to other countries. Uzbekistan and Kyrgyzstan are the most likely first victims of such a scenario, owing to their common ethnic structure with Tajikistan. Alternatively, a local conflict could drag its neighboring countries into a war. For example, the rise of a new conflict or the expansion of the existing armed conflict in either Kyrgyzstan's, Uzbekistan's, or Tajikistan's part of the Ferghana Valley could expand to the other two neighbors. This was experienced in 2000 when a war engulfed the entire Ferghana Valley. Such conflict would inevitably drag the three neighbors into a long war of attrition against the valley's armed groups, for an unpredictable length of time but with imaginable extensive destruction. As a possibility, the rise of Uzbek nationalism could also provoke a war in Central Asia. If fully pursued, it will provoke militarist nationalism in its three neighbors—Kazakhstan, Kyrgyzstan, and Tajikistan—to kindle major territorial and ethnic disputes in these countries. Thanks to the Soviet drawing of borders, the three countries have territorial claims against each other. In such a situation, territorial claims raised by Uzbekistan or any other regional country will be responded to by claims by the others. The result will be catastrophic for all of them, as territorial claims could drag the region into a long and violent territorial conflict. Finally, the resumption of civil war in Afghanistan and its spillover into Central Asia, a realistic possibility despite the fall of the Taliban and the establishment of an interim government in Afghanistan, could ignite a civil war in any neighboring CA country (Tajikistan, Turkmenistan, or Uzbekistan). In turn, this could expand to others for the reasons mentioned earlier.

The regional powers sharing borders with Central Asia cannot remain indifferent in the event of the outbreak of any major military conflict in their neighboring countries. Many factors will motivate China, Iran, and Russia to intervene and will determine the extent of their intervention. The most important are the intensity of the conflict, its speed of expansion, its predictable impact on each of them, the degree of importance of the affected countries for the regional powers, and the latter's level of commitment to those countries. Concerned about the expansion of independence movements in its Xinjiang Province, China will have every reason for containing a military conflict along its long borders with Kazakhstan, Kyrgyzstan, and Tajikistan, whether it is in the form of a civil war or an interstate war. Such conflict could expand to China because of the existing ethnic ties. At a minimum, it could further radicalize the Uyghur independence movements. For the same reason, any conflict in Uzbekistan and Tajikistan with the potential to expand to other countries would make China concerned. At the June 2001 Shanghai Cooperation Organisation meeting, the Chinese expressed their fear of the growing independence movement in Xinjiang and of the growth of extremism in Afghanistan, which could destabilize all of Central Asia and the neighboring Chinese province.[57] China's agreement with the other participants on the necessity of a common policy to fight terrorism and extremism clearly indicated its seriousness about the threat and its willingness to take action should the need arise. Besides, China's extensive economic relations with Kazakhstan and Kyrgyzstan have created an economic stake for the Chinese in the stability of their neighbors.

Iran will also have its own reasons for engagement in any major conflict. There is no ethnic or independence movement in Iran. However, the existence in Iran of an ethnic Turkmen minority of about 500,000 people living along the Iranian-Turkmen border creates a potential for the expansion of instability from Turkmenistan into Iran. This potential threat aside, Iran should be worried about the consequences of any major military conflict in Central Asia, with which Iran shares about 1,500 kilometers of border. As a major conceivable scenario, a civil war in Central Asia could lead to an inflow of small arms and refugees, with both security and economic implications for

Iran. Since 1978, that country has experienced firsthand the same problems because of the Afghan civil war, the negative impact of which on Iran has continued despite the end of the full-scale civil war and the creation of an interim government in Afghanistan. War and instability in Afghanistan have created major security threats for Iran along its long border with Afghanistan. Therefore, the Iranians have had strong concerns about any major instability in their neighboring countries posing additional security threats for them. Iran might also be dragged into a CA war because of its commitment to certain countries. As a guarantor of the 1997 Tajik peace accord, Iran is committed along with Russia to the compliance with the accord of the two parties to the conflict.[58] For this reason or for defending the Tajiks with whom the Iranians have ethnic, linguistic, and historical links, Iran could feel obliged to enter a war or civil war involving Tajikistan. This could—and, in the case of a war between Tajikistan and Uzbekistan, would—lead to a major regional military conflict. Iran has a security accord with Kyrgyzstan which forbids the use of the territory of the two countries for hostile activities against each other.[59] For that matter, Iran might also be forced to assist Kyrgyzstan if its security is threatened. The details of the agreement are not publicized. However, Iran's commitment to its security in the case of war could be a realistic component, although it may not be compelled to assist it in the case of a civil war.

Finally, Iran might also be dragged into a military conflict involving Turkmenistan, the only CA country with a very long common border with Iran. One reason could be Iran's fear of the spillover of instability from that country into Iran, as this could immediately affect the Iranian province of Golestan, which is dominated by ethnic Turkmen. Another reason could be its close ties with the Turkmen, whose multidimensional relations with Iran have been growing steadily. Apart from economic, political, social, and cultural relations, there are also the military and security agreements concluded in the 1990s.[60] Accordingly, Iran has been helping the Turkmen military with both training and equipment. It is not known whether these agreements also oblige Iran to assist the Turkmen government in the case of a war of any nature. Even if this were not so, Iran's extensive, multidimensional ties with that country would create a large enough stake for the Iranians in the stability of Turkmenistan.[61] In addition, its geographical position as Iran's only land link to Central Asia would create an even stronger stake for them. In short, many factors will likely force Iran to become involved in a major military conflict in that region.

Like Iran, Russia will likely find it difficult to remain indifferent to a major military conflict in Central Asia. The existence of Russian troops in that region as part of Russia's various defense agreements with the CA countries has created the capability for it to engage in military operations in the region.[62] Apart from Uzbekistan, which has its own border patrols, the Russian forces have patrolled the international borders of the CA countries with Iran, China, and Afghanistan since the early 1990s.[63] Russia considers such borders as it own southern borders.[64] In addition to the border troops, the Russians have kept some of the Soviet military bases in Tajikistan. They have been involved in limited military operations in the region since the early 1990s, and during the Tajik civil war they supplied arms to the Tajik government. Russian troops also fought with the Afghanistan-based Tajik opposition groups and their Afghan Mujahedin allies operating against the Tajik government forces in the Afghan-Tajik border areas. As agreed with the Tajik government, the Russian border guards have patrolled Tajikistan's border with Afghanistan since the early 1990s. In that capacity, they have been engaged in low-key fighting with drug-traffickers operating from Afghanistan who are trying to enter Tajikistan on their way to Central Asia, Russia, and Europe.

The rise and/or expansion of extremism and terrorism in Central Asia will likely provoke Russia's military involvement in that region. In fact, it has expressed concern about these phenomena since the fall of the Soviet Union. The Russian government has exaggerated their threat in order to justify its reestablishment there. Nevertheless, it has also been genuinely concerned about the threat. The rise of extremism in Central Asia could create tension along Russia's southern borders, with the possibility of expansion into it over time. There are various non-Russian ethnic groups, both large and small, in Russia with strong reasons for dissatisfaction with the government. Their existence has created grounds for Russia's fear of their radicalization as a result of tensions and military conflicts in neighboring Central Asia. Symbolically, Chechnya has demonstrated the possibility of such a scenario with dire consequences for the territorial integrity of Russia. Fear of its duplication was one of the reasons for Russia's military support of the Tajik government during the Tajik civil war. The long Afghan civil war, which lasted in its full-scale form until the fall of the

Taliban in 2001, and the continuation of instability and uncertainty in post-Taliban Afghanistan, a situation conducive to the resumption of the civil war, have posed a major security threat in the entire West Asia. They have worsened Russia's concerns about the expansion of extremism in Central Asia.

The possibility of the "export" of extremism from Afghanistan to Central Asia—still a realistic scenario given the fragility of the situation in Afghanistan under its interim government—and the radicalization of the region have made the Russians especially worried. As discussed earlier, fear of this scenario motivated them to take steps in early 2001 for forming a rapid-reaction force with Armenia and certain CA countries.[65] It has also inclined them to work with China and the CA countries, excluding Turkmenistan, as part of the Shanghai Cooperation Organization.[66] Taking into consideration all these factors, it is logical to conclude that Russia will almost certainly enter regional conflicts involving extremists. The intensity of the threat will determine its form of intervention, which may range from supplying arms to the affected countries to direct involvement of Russian military forces. The fact that it has been active in both areas since the early 1990s makes its future resort to such activities not a surprise. However, its direct involvement in regional conflicts has been limited so far. This limitation will likely disappear in the future, given the growing anxiety in the region and Russia about extremism. Russia's increasing worry about its disintegration has also made it concerned about the activities of internal extremist groups and those in the proximity of its borders and whether these would stay inactive in the case of a major military conflict in Central Asia. In view of this, in the near future Russia might find itself deeply engaged in a regional war, a war whose development and end could not be determined by any single government actor.

The regional powers neighboring Central Asia (Iran, China, and Russia) might also be dragged into a military conflict to prevent the domination of the region by a rival power. Fear of loss of political influence or economic gain as a result of the gradual monopolization of one of them could provoke the others' aggressive involvement to deny or limit gains to the other/others. China's interests in Central Asia have so far been centered on Kazakhstan and Kyrgyzstan. Its interests have been mainly economic, but with a growing security interest because of the increasing ethnic problems in its Xinjiang province. China needs a long period of peace to complete its economic transitional period and address its underdevelopment. This reality has made it quite cautious in regional and international affairs. For this reason, its extensive military involvement in the region will be an unlikely scenario in the foreseeable future unless the rise of extremism there and particularly in its neighboring CA countries leaves it with no choice but to move in to stop eastward expansion into its territory. The intensity of such phenomenon in Central Asia and the strength of independence movement in Xinjiang will determine China's extent, duration, and intensity of military involvement.

Unlike China, Iran and Russia have long-term multidimensional interests in all of Eurasia. Their common interests have pushed them together to work in concert in that region. The most important of these interests are their stake in the stability of Central Asia and the Caucasus, their concern about Afghanistan, and their fear of the extensive presence of a nonregional power (United States), its ally (Turkey), and a hostile military alliance (NATO) along their borders. Their extensive economic relations, dissatisfaction with the existing international order, and opposition to attempts for the creation of a unipolar American-led international system have created additional reasons for their cooperation. These factors have prevented their hostile rivalry in Central Asia and the Caucasus—that is, they have refrained from attempting to eliminate each other's influence. Nonetheless, Iran and Russia have been engaged in clear political and economic competition with each other and also with Turkey.[67] Their common regional and international interests will likely restrain their regional rivalry for a while, but this situation—caused by their political, economic, and military weaknesses and vulnerability to third parties—may not last forever. Whichever of the two countries overcomes its restrictive shortcomings first will find little incentive to tolerate the other's growing interests. That could develop into a direct military confrontation or a proxy war fought by their protégés. Finally, any Chinese effort to expand in Central Asia at the expense of either or both countries will also provoke a hostile reaction to China, possibly of a military form.

The United States, a country with clear political and economic interests in the Caspian region, could also be dragged into a military conflict in Central Asia or the Caucasus. As a nonregional country, the most conceivable circumstances under which this scenario could happen would be in the event of a threat to its economic interests. These mainly relate to the oil and natural-gas resources of the three Caspian countries, Azerbaijan, Kazakhstan, and Turkmenistan. However, certain realities will in practice rule out its direct involvement in the form of dispatching troops to engage in full-scale military operations in the Caucasus and Central Asia. To start with, as a nonregional country with no common border with the two regions, its participation in any future military conflict would require the consent of the countries in the vicinity of these regions or the affected regional countries themselves. As it neighbors the Caucasus, Turkey is the only realistic candidate for hosting American forces. The United States already has a few military bases there, including an airforce base in Dyar Baker, the Inchirlik airbase, and at least two listening bases. However, it is highly unlikely that the Turks will allow a massive concentration of American forces in their territory for any major operation in the Caucasus or Central Asia. One reason is the growing popular opposition to the presence of American forces in Turkey, and the continued operation of the existing American bases in that country has been questioned. The Turkish government has expressed this opposition by hinting at the possibility of not renewing the contract for the use of its Inchirlik airbase. Another reason for Turkey's refusal to assist the Americans would be its well-founded fear of a military reaction by Iran and Russia. They would undoubtedly not tolerate the heavy military presence of the United States along or in the vicinity of their borders. Apart from these factors, geographical realities will also limit the options for the Americans. Turkey borders with Armenia, Georgia, and the Azeri territory of the Nakhjevan Autonomous Republic, separated from Azerbaijan by the Armenian territory. As it is sandwiched between Iran and Armenia, the latter is out of the question as a foothold for any American military operation. As a close ally of Russia, a good friend of Iran, and an enemy of Turkey, Armenia will not allow the presence of American forces in its territory or their passage through its land or air space to access Azerbaijan or the Central Asian countries.

Georgia has sought NATO membership and close ties with the United States. Theoretically, this makes it an ideal country to cooperate with the Americans in any military operations in the Caucasus. Nevertheless, the realities will make such cooperation practically an impossible scenario. Without a doubt, Russia will not tolerate the extensive presence of American forces along its southern borders with

Georgia. Nor will it tolerate any major American military intervention in its former republics, which would have inevitably security implications for Russia. The Russians have the capability to punish the Georgian government in the case of its cooperation with any American military operation in or through the Caucasus. It has large concentrations of military forces in its three North Caucasian republics of Chechnya, Inghushetia, and Dagestan along the Georgian and Azeri borders. Additionally, it has military bases inside Georgia (e.g., one in Akhalkalaki in the Javakhetia region and another in Batumi in the Ajaria region). Finally, Russia has the capability to dismember Georgia through its manipulation of its separatist movements. These facts have convinced the Georgian government to hint at a change of mind regarding its NATO membership. In early 2001, President Sheverdnadzhe expressed an interest in turning Georgia into a neutral state instead of seeking NATO membership.[68]

If Georgia's Black Sea ports create at least a theoretical feasibility for sending American troops to the Caucasus despite Turkey's lack of cooperation, accessing the land-locked Central Asia for the Americans is an almost impossible mission. The region is accessible via land through its neighbors—Iran, China, and Russia—but undoubtedly none of these will assist America with its military operations to affect the pace of events in Central Asia. Central Asia is also accessible via the Caucasus and the Caspian Sea, located between the two regions. Yet, accessing it through the Caucasus will bring about the impediments mentioned previously. These facts will make very unrealistic a significant deployment of American forces in Central Asia without provoking a military confrontation with Russia and Iran.

Given the barriers mentioned, indirect involvement will be the only feasible type of involvement for the United States in any future major military conflict if it does not wish to engage itself in a major war with the three regional powers (Iran, China, Russia) or any of them. Supplying arms and intelligence as well as financial assistance would be the major conceivable options. Yet there are also limits on arms supplying. Any significant assistance or sale of military hardware to a Caucasian or CA country which had a major impact on the balance of power in its respective region would provoke a hostile reaction by regional neighbors weakened or threatened by the transaction. In addition, such a development would also result in a harsh response by Russia and Iran, which would likely assess it as a clear threat to their security. In

June 2001, the supply of military boats by America to Azerbaijan, described by them as coastal patrol boats with no weapon systems, provoked a harsh reaction by Turkmenistan.[69] Having tense relations with Azerbaijan over the division of their offshore resources in the Caspian Sea, including the Serdar oilfield (called Kyapaz by the Azeris),[70] Turkmenistan interpreted the transaction as a clear military threat to its country. The Turkmen responded by revealing their purchase of Ukrainian military boats.[71] Sharing land and sea borders with Azerbaijan, Iran also expressed concern about the development and evaluated it as a move toward upsetting the balance of power in the Caspian Sea.[72]

NOTES

1. Paata Zakareishvili, "An Open Wound," Institute for War & Peace Reporting, Caucasus Reporting Service, No. 15b, 24 January 2000 (internet publication).

2. Hooman Peimani, *The Caspian Pipeline Dilemma: Political Games and Economic Losses* (Westport, CT: Praeger, 2001), 88.

3. "Georgia: UN Envoy Hopes Abkhaz Status Talks Follow Yalta Success," REF/RL, 22 March 2001.

4. Ibid.

5. Jean-Christophe Peuch, "Georgia: Little Hope Seen for Abkhaz Peace Process," REF/RL, 4 May 2001.

6. Robert McMahon, "Georgia: UN Envoy Hopes Abkhaz Status Talks Follow Yalta Success," RFE/RL, 22 March 2001.

7. Ibid.

8. Jean-Christophe Peuch, "Caucasus: Georgia Sees Future in Regional Cooperation," RFE/RL, 18 May 2001.

9. Peimani, *The Caspian Pipeline Dilemma*, 88.

10. REF/RL web journal, "Transcaucasia and Central Asia," 29 May 2001.

11. For a detailed account on the merits and shortcomings of the available oil-export routes for the Caspian countries and on the reasons behind the American opposition to the use of Iran and Russia as export routes, see Peimani, *The Caspian Pipeline Dilemma,* 73–112.

12. For details of Iran's swap deals, see ibid., 61–62.

13. Hojatolah Faghani, "The Eastward Expansion of NATO: A Review of the Georgia's Position," *Majelieh-e Motaellat-e Asyaie Markazi va Ghafghaz* [*Central Asia and the Caucasus Review*] (Tehran), No. 26 (Summer 1999), 28.

14. "Meeting Between Armenian, Azerbaijani Presidents Postponed," REF/RL, 29 May 2001.

15. Institute for War & Peace Reporting, Caucasus Reporting Service, Vol. 9, No. 6, 9 June 2000 (internet publication).

16. Ibid.

17. Ibid.

18. Ibid.

19. Ibid.

20. Ibid.

21. RFE/RL, "Transcaucasia and Central Asia," 29 May 2001.

22. Ibid.

23. Ibid.

24. "Newsline," RFE/RL, 13 June 2001.

25. Hooman Peimani, "Drug-Trafficking in the Ferghana Valley and Instability in Central Asia," *The Times of Central Asia* (Bishkek), 2 November 2000, 8.

26. Ibid.

27. Ibid.

28. Bruce Pannier, "Uzbekistan: Human Rights Watch Calls Tashkent Trials Unfair," REF/RL, 4 June 2001.

29. Bruce Pannier, "Central Asia: Shanghai Cooperation Organisation Ends Summit," REF/RL, 15 June 2001.

30. Ibid.

31. Ibid.

32. Ibid.

33. Valery Shaldiz, "The Ossetian Crisis in Georgia," *Majelieh-e Motaellat-e Asyaie Markazi va Ghafghaz* [*Central Asia and the Caucasus Review*] (Tehran), 2, No. 1 (Summer 1993), 163–168.

34. For details, see Bahram Amirahmadian, "The Trend of Developments in the Karabakh Crisis," *Majelieh-e Motaellat-e Asyaie Markazi va Ghafghaz* [*Central Asia and the Caucasus Review*] (Tehran), 28 (Winter 2000), 27–50.

35. Roland Dannreuther, "Russia, Central Asia and the Persian Gulf," *Survival*, 35, No. 4 (Winter 1993–94), 102.

36. "Tajikistan: Introductory Survey," in *The Europa World Year Book 1994* (London: Europa, 1994), 2752.

37. Bruce Pannier, "Central Asia: Border Dispute between Uzbekistan and Kyrgyzstan Risks Triggering Conflict," REF/RL, 8 March 1999.

38. Ibid.

39. For information on pollution of the Aral Sea and its devastating impact on Kazakhstan and Uzbekistan, see Michael Fergus, "The Aral Sea Environmental Crisis: Problems and a Way Forward," *Asian Affairs*, 30, No. 1 (February 1999), 35–44; Max Spoor, "The Aral Sea Basin Crisis: Transition and

Environment in Former Soviet Central Asia," *Development and Change*, 29, No. 3 (July 1998), 409–435; Gassem Maleki, "The Aral Sea: An Environmental Crisis," *Majelieh-e Motaellat-e Asyaie Markazi va Ghafghaz [Central Asia and the Caucasus Review]* (Tehran), 26 (Summer 1999), 53–66.

40. Igor Ratter, "Will Central Asia Explode?" *Journal of Central Asia and Caucasian Review*, 2, No. 1 (Summer 1993), 197.

41. Ibid.

42. Ibid.

43. Peimani, "Drug-Trafficking in the Ferghana Valley and Instability in Central Asia," *The Times of Central Asia* (Bishkek), 2 November 2000, 8.

44. For an account on the factors shaping the interests of Iran, China, Turkey, and Russia, see: Hooman Peimani, *Regional Security and the Future of Central Asia: The Competition of Iran, Turkey, and Russia* (Westport, CT: Praeger, 1998), 23–128.

45. For a detailed analysis of the interest of Iran, China, Turkey, and Russia in the Caspian oil industry, see Peimani, *The Caspian Pipeline Dilemma*, 73–112.

46. For an account on the significance of the Caspian energy resources for the United States, see ibid., 23–30.

47. Abulfazel Elchibey died in 2000 in Turkey. For general information on his political life, see "Azerbaijan," *Eurasian File* (Ankara), 133 (August 2000), 3–4.

48. For details on Turkey's political and economic advancement in Central Asia and the Caucasus in the early 1990s, see Peimani, *Regional Security and the Future of Central Asia*, 47–52, 84–86, and 95–100.

49. Peimani, *Regional Security and the Future of Central Asia*, 49–50.

50. Hooman Peimani, *Iran and the United States: The Rise of the West Asian Regional Grouping* (Westport, CT: Praeger, 2000), 35–38.

51. Michael Lelyveld, "Caspian: U.S. Says Patrol Boats Are Gifts to Promote Regional Security," REF/RL, 26 June 2001.

52. For a detailed account on various issues pertaining to the Baku–Ceyhan pipeline, see Peimani, *The Caspian Pipeline Dilemma:* 77–108.

53. Peuch, "Caucasus."

54. For a comprehensive analysis of factors weakening Georgia's position as long-term export route for the Caspian oil exports, see: Peimani, *The Caspian Pipeline Dilemma*, 50–54.

55. Peimani, *Regional Security and the Future of Central Asia*, 76.

56. Ibid., 30, 67.

57. Bruce Pannier, "Central Asia: Shanghai Cupertino Organisation Ends Summit," REF/RL, 15 June 2001.

58. Peimani, *Iran and the United States*, 31.

59. Peimani, *Regional Security and the Future of Central Asia*, 84.

60. Ibid., 83.

61. For an analysis of Iran's growing ties with Turkmenistan, see: Peimani, *Iran and the United States*, 27–30.

62. For an account on Russia's military agreements with the Central Asian countries, see Peimani, *Regional Security and the Future of Central Asia,*, 75–77.

63. Ibid., 76.

64. Renee de Nevers, "Russia's Strategic Renovation," *Adelphi Paper,* 289 (July 1994), 44–45.

65. RFE/RL, "Transcaucasia and Central Asia," 29 May 2001.

66. Pannier, "Central Asia."

67. For a detailed analysis of the different aspects of the rivalry among Iran, Turkey, and Russia in Eurasia, see Peimani, *Regional Security and the Future of Central Asia.*

68. Peuch, "Caucasus."

69. Lelyveld, "Caspian."

70. Peimani, *The Caspian Pipeline Dilemma,* 41–42.

71. Lelyveld, "Caspian."

72. Ibid.

6

Conclusion

The fall of the USSR imposed a transitional process on the former Soviet republics. During the first decade of independence, almost all of them have proven unable to tackle their numerous economic, political, and social problems. Among them, the worst case has been that of the countries of the Caucasus and Central Asia. Azerbaijan, Armenia, and Georgia, as well as Kazakhstan, Kyrgyzstan, Tajikistan, Turkmenistan, and Uzbekistan, have all failed to address most of the major problems that surfaced at the time of independence. Their record of economic achievements has been particularly disappointing. Even though there have been differences among them in terms of extent of economic recovery, they have not experienced any real or significant growth. This is also true for the three major oil and gas exporters (Azerbaijan, Kazakhstan, and Turkmenistan). At the time of independence, they expected to become within a decade as prosperous as Kuwait. There are practically no grounds to believe that they can achieve that level of prosperity even a decade from now. With few exceptions, the expansion of the economies of the Caucasian and CA countries has been dwarfed by their contraction, which was very substantial during the first few years of independence. Those few countries (i.e., Armenia and Uzbekistan) with economic growth beyond recovery to the level of their preindependence era have registered only sluggish rates of GDP expansion. Given the depth of the

economic shortcomings of these countries, shared also by their regional neighbors, the limited growth has been too insignificant to have
a noticeable positive impact on their respective countries. All the
Caucasian and CA countries require years, if not decades, of economic
growth at large rates to overcome their immediate problems and address their underdevelopment. There is no evidence that this necessary
process is about to start in the foreseeable future. If the current trend
continues, all eight Caucasian and CA countries will likely face severe
economic difficulties with dire social and political consequences.

Poor economic performance has had a major social impact. The fall
of the Soviet Union led to a sudden lowering of the living standards of
the Caucasians and the Central Asians. This phenomenon arose because of their previous heavy dependency on Moscow's assistance in
cash and kind, which was cut in 1991. Their limited indigenous
resources and the dismal economic situation of the postindependence
era have further lowered their living standards. The latter has also
resulted in growing unemployment and poverty, with further worsening effects on their overall welfare. The Caucasian and CA governments have not had adequate means to tackle all these agonizing
phenomena. As an indicator of the postindependence failure, no viable
economic private sector has emerged. In its absence, the public sector
has been simply unable to generate an adequate number of well-paid
long-term jobs to address unemployment and poverty. The limited
means of the Caucasian and CA governments have also resulted in a
significant reduction in the preindependence social and health services
which were available to everyone as a means to ensure minimum
living standards for the Soviet people. The loss of such privileges has
further worsened the situation for average Caucasians and Central
Asians, who are unable to meet their basic needs with their limited
incomes. In such a situation, the poor record of their governments in
solving various social and economic problems has disillusioned them
about the possibility of change for the better in the near future. All
these factors have contributed to a growing dissatisfaction among the
Caucasians and Central Asians, most of whom have had a hard time
meeting their basic needs.

If the economic record of the three Caucasian and five CA countries
has been disappointing, their political record has not been very different. The initial hope of their peoples to establish democratic political

systems in the postindependence era was dashed when almost immediately after independence most of their leaders opted for undemocratic regimes. These authoritarian political systems are, in essence, the old Soviet system without its guiding ideological objectives. They have taken somewhat different forms from the old system to make them compatible with the realities of the new era and with the peculiar characteristics of each country. Along this line, they have now become nationalist institutions led by the old Soviet political elite turned nationalists.

Despite superficial differences, the Caucasian and CA political systems have in practice continued the style of governance used in the Soviet era. By and large, they have pursued the policy of intolerance of political dissent in any form, whether by political groups or by individuals. Their leaders and governments rule without accountability to any organ and with impunity. Their ruling elites have ensured their continued rule through their abuse of the political system and its institutions. Elections at all levels have become ceremonial means for legitimizing the already hand-picked persons. The existing political systems have been dictatorial institutions run by despotic leaders. Besides abuse of power, widespread corruption has been a defining characteristic of the postindependence Caucasian and CA political systems. This has also been the case in the so-called democratic countries—namely, Kazakhstan and Kyrgyzstan. What has made the latter somewhat different from their Caucasian and CA counterparts has been their tolerance of a degree of personal freedoms and rights for their nationals. However, they have gradually shifted to the "mainstream" over the last few years as reflected in their style of statecraft. In short, all the Caucasian and CA ruling elites have over time opted for authoritarianism. This now seems more appropriate for their weakened and challenged authority and for the continuity of their political institutions through a long and unpredictable transitional period.

The growing dissatisfaction among the Caucasians and Central Asians has created suitable grounds for the rise of dissent in various forms. Lowering living standards, rising unemployment, and poverty have made them dissatisfied with the present state of affairs. Added to this, the rampant corruption among their ruling circles and a prevailing undemocratic environment have made them disillusioned about the ability of their leaders and their political systems to address the enormous transitional problems. This situation has paved the way for the emergence of popular dissatisfaction and political discontent in organized and unorganized forms.

Fearful of this destabilizing possibility, all their leaders have found authoritarianism as a "guarantee" for the continuity of their rule and the stability of their political systems. Concerns about the rise of ethnic movements in their multiethnic countries have created another incentive for their resort to this kind of political system. The latter has been a major justification for their shift to despotic and intolerant forms of government. Many of the Caucasian and CA governments (Azerbaijan, Armenia, Georgia, and Tajikistan) have experienced violent ethnic conflicts, with devastating effects on their countries. Others have had grounds to be fearful of the rise of such phenomena in their countries despite the absence of such problems in their postindependence era.

Apart from internal factors, certain external factors have further convinced these governments of the merits of authoritarianism. Radical ethnic movements in countries in their proximity or in those neighboring their regions have certainly alarmed them. The ethnic makeup of the Caucasian and CA countries makes the expansion of ethnic movements in violent and nonviolent forms from one country to another a feasible scenario. The existence of the same ethnic groups on both sides of the borders between Central Asia and their neighboring China and Afghanistan has also created a potential for the expansion of an ethnic conflict (China) and a civil war (Afghanistan) to the CA countries. In particular, the continuation of instability in Afghanistan has created a well-founded anxiety, which has lasted in the post-Taliban era as the overall situation in Afghanistan has created grounds for a new round of civil war. Civil war and instability in that country could potentially even radicalize the ethnic minorities of Russia and is thus a concern for the Russians, who have also used it as a pretext for their return to their former CA republics. Besides this political incentive, it is a fact that instability in the Caucasus and Central Asia neighboring Russia could expand to that country and vice versa. Until the fall of the Taliban, China's fear of the expansion of extremism and terrorism from Taliban-dominated Afghanistan to its troubled Xinjiang Province via its neighboring Central Asia also had realistic grounds. In the absence of the Taliban, the persistence of political uncertainty in Afghanistan should still make the Chinese fearful of the spillover of instability and extremism, as dissatisfied Afghan groups could resume the civil war—an undesirable but still feasible scenario. The shared fear of expansion of instability have justified cooperation among most of the Caucasian and CA countries with China and Russia within the context of the CIS collective security agreement and also that of the Shanghai Cooperation Organization.

The eight countries of the Caucasus and Central Asia have become prone to the rise of instability in different forms. On the one hand, the growing dissatisfaction among their peoples has prepared grounds for the emergence of political opposition in different forms, including popular dissent targeting the very existence of their political regimes. Needless to say, this is an ideal environment for the rise and growth of extremist groups to take the lead in such eruptions of dissent. The worsening overall situation in those countries will gradually make their peoples interested in extremist political views that sound more in tune with their situation than those of their ruling elites. This situation will likely lead to violent political activities, matched by violence by the challenged regimes. The result could well be armed conflicts, including civil war. On the other hand, the unresolved ethnic conflicts especially in the Caucasus have created a tense situation that could lead to the rekindling of ethnic violence. Unless the root causes of ethnic strife in Azerbaijan and Georgia are resolved peacefully—an unrealistic possibility in the near future—there is little doubt that the current deadlock will give birth to a new round of civil wars in those countries. In Central Asia, the three countries sharing the Ferghana Valley could be dragged into a civil war. In addition to the existence of armed groups in the valley, these multiethnic countries have other sources of internal strife capable of developing into civil wars.

In both cases, the resort of the Caucasian and CA leaders to nationalism, and most probably to its extremist versions, will likely further worsen the situation. To be used as an alternative ideology to disenchanted peoples already vulnerable to extremist ideologies, extreme nationalism based on the superiority of one's ethnic group in a multiethnic country can hardly help strengthen a political system challenged by other extremists. On the contrary, it will provoke animosity and insecurity on the part of the other ethnic groups. It will also encourage the hostility of neighboring countries, which may feel threatened by the rising nationalism. Other sources of hostility between these countries such as existing territorial or border disputes could well lead to wars between and among them. The precedence for the use of force for changing borders and settling border disputes leaves no doubt about the feasibility of such a bleak scenario.

Given the circumstances mentioned, the countries of the Caucasus and Central Asia are likely heading toward military conflicts. Unless the current trend is reversed, civil or interstate wars will be on the horizon at least for most of them. However, these destructive events are not new to the two regions. In fact, they both experienced wars and civil wars during the first few years of independence. The obvious human suffering and destructive nature of the events aside, what makes the situation alarming this time is the strong possibility for the expansion of hostilities well beyond their initial boundaries. For a variety of reasons, civil wars in the two regions could escalate to interstate wars pitting one regional country against its neighbor or neighbors. Among others, certain factors could escalate an interstate war into a regional war engulfing and/or affecting their respective region for an unpredictable period of time. Ethnic commonalities and territorial and border disputes between the countries at war and other regional countries are two imaginable factors.

A regional war may even further escalate as a result of the intentional or unintentional involvement of four regional (Iran, China, Turkey, and Russia) and one nonregional (United States) powers. These five states have long-term interests in all or some of the Caucasian and/or CA countries, giving them stakes in the security and stability of their respective regions. For one reason or another, they could be dragged into any future regional military conflicts should their long-term interests seem threatened. Alternatively, they could become involved through defense of the interests of a regional country to which they are committed for economic, political, or security reasons. Many factors will determine the type and extent of their intervention in any future military conflict—that is, whether such intervention will be direct or indirect. Regardless of its form, this type of escalation will further deteriorate the situation and deepen the military conflict by upsetting the balance of power in favor of or against one country or another. In this case, the expansion and the deepening of a regional war will surely bring about dire consequences for all involved as well as for the immediate region. However, the direct involvement of any of them in the form of dispatching troops will escalate the conflict to a dangerous level. Such escalation could provoke a reaction in kind by other powers. The accessibility of the war zone to the concerned power or powers and the nature of threat to their interests and those of their friends and allies in the war-affected region would determine whether they could take action as well.

Conceivable scenarios such as these would potentially contain the possibility of a military confrontation between and among Iran, China, Turkey, Russia, and the United States. Of the five, the direct involvement of the United States is the least likely possibility. As a non-regional country, its massive direct involvement would be almost impossible. Apart from technical issues hampering such an undertaking, direct American engagement in a conflict in Central Asia or the Caucasus would certainly provoke a hostile reaction by both Iran and Russia. It is not conceivable that they would remain indifferent to the extensive concentration of American military forces in a region with which they share long borders. Their efforts since the collapse of the Soviet Union to keep nonregional powers, and especially the United States, and NATO out of the two regions have left no doubt about their military response and most probably joint action to remove the potential source of threat from their vicinity. Needless to say, this confrontation would be a development whose implications would go far beyond the Caucasus or Central Asia, whichever the case may be.

China would be the next least likely candidate for a direct military involvement. To start with, its direct engagement would only be feasible in Central Asia, with which it has a long border. In this case, its concern about a destructive impact of severe tension in Kazakhstan, Kyrgyzstan, and Tajikistan on its troubled Xinjiang Province could potentially make it inclined to send troops. China's need for a long period of peace to complete its economic transition has made it extremely cautious. It is highly unlikely that it would engage itself militarily in a conflict in Central Asia for any purpose other than its fear of the dismemberment of Xinjiang Province.

Turkey's direct involvement would in practice be limited to the Caucasus, for geographical realities. Given the sensitivity of Iran and Russia to the deployment of troops in that region by a NATO member, the expected military response by the two countries to such a development would be a major factor weakening its likelihood in the foreseeable future.

Iran and Russia are more likely to intervene in a major military conflict in the Caucasus or Central Asia. Sharing long borders with both regions, they would be worried about the impact of any such conflict on their security, for at least three reasons. First, their ethnic, religious, and historical ties with those regions make the spillover of such conflicts into their countries a very feasible scenario. At a minimum, they would expect the inflow of refugees and arms into their countries, with both economic and security implications. Second, the possibility of the intentional or unintentional engagement of their friends or allies in any regional military conflict, with direct economic and security implications for them, would probably motivate their intervention to prevent its escalation. Finally, as a major war in the Caucasus or Central Asia would create a potential environment for the direct presence of Turkey and/or the United States in either of those regions, Iran and Russia would have no hesitation to eliminate that potential. Their direct involvement would therefore be aimed at ending the conflict or at its containment in order to deny to the Turks or the Americans the opportunity for deploying their forces.

The Caucasians and the Central Asians began their era of independence with an expectation for building a better and more prosperous future than was their past. The first decade of independence has failed to meet this expectation. Wars in different forms and intensity have marked the independence era. The last decade of the twentieth century offered wars to the Azeris, the Armenians, the Georgians, and the Tajiks. Unless the current pace of events is stopped, the first decade of the twenty-first century will likely offer them and most of the other peoples of Central Asia more destructive and extensive wars, with devastating impact on their social and economic development. There are internal and external factors that will likely contribute to the instigation of wars of different forms. Yet a major contributing factor has been the declining economy of virtually all the eight Caucasian and CA countries. The resulting lowering living standards, growing unemployment, and expanding poverty have created a situation in these countries conducive to the rise of conflict in different forms. Such a development can not only destabilize those countries, but can also initiate a process that will contribute to interstate conflicts. The rise of nationalism in response to the emerging domestic conflicts in a Caucasian or CA country will provoke hostility in its neighbors, with the possibility of its escalation to military confrontation among them. Tackling economic problems should therefore become the major preventive measure.

However, there is little, if any, hope for a significant change in the economies of the Caucasian and CA countries, including those of the oil and natural-gas exporters. In all these countries, the absence of an adequate amount of foreign assistance has put the financial burden for any type of economic activity on their governments, which have very limited domestic resources. There is no indication of a major change in this situation in the near future. Given their numerous transitional challenges, depth of underdevelopment, and limited resources, it will take the Caucasian and CA countries at least a decade to overcome their current dismal economic status. Because of their small available resources, the process might well be much longer for nonenergy exporters.

This disappointing economic forecast leaves little room for optimism regarding the possibility of avoiding military conflicts in Central Asia and the Caucasus, at least in the short run. Of course, this bleak prediction is confined to conflicts driven by internal factors. Yet it is quite feasible, though of course not easy, to eliminate or at least limit the influence of external factors that could also contribute to instability and war. For one, the end of the civil war in Afghanistan, if followed by a successful stabilization program, will eliminate the threat of its expansion to its neighboring CA countries—Tajikistan, Turkmenistan, and Uzbekistan. By offering a safe heaven to international drug-traffickers, Afghanistan under the Taliban posed a major threat to the security of Central Asia. Despite the toppling of the Taliban regime in 2001, drug production and drug-trafficking have continued. The use of arms by the drug-traffickers to secure their passage to Russia via Central Asia has been a major source of threat to the security of all CA countries on the drug route—that is, all the CA countries excluding Turkmenistan. The extensive war in the Ferghana Valley in 2000 demonstrated the intensity of the threat. Hence, the restoration of peace and stability in Afghanistan will be a prerequisite for long-term stability in that region and particularly in Kyrgyzstan, Tajikistan, and Uzbekistan. The formation of the Afghan interim government, if it survives, is just a first step toward those objectives. Appreciating the depth of threat, the CA countries have joined China and Russia to deal with Afghan-based drug-traffickers and to prevent the spillover of war, terrorism, and extremism from Afghanistan. If they move beyond diplomatic statements and limited cooperation, their efforts could, and will likely, complement those of other countries threatened over time by the ills of the Afghan civil war. The latter have also sought regional cooperation. Iranian–Russian cooperation supported by India to stabilize Afghanistan has been a well-known case. This type of cooperation has taken place both within the UN-sponsored 6+2 Group, consisting of six neighbors of Afghanistan as well as the United States and Russia outside the group as part of joint actions of the two states with common security interests in their proximity. In the post-Taliban era, one should hope that the collective efforts of the Central Asian states and those of others threatened by the Afghan civil war should suffice to help the efforts of the Afghans, under the leadership of their interim government, to end once and forever over two decades of civil war, which still continues at a low level, by eliminating its root causes. Their persistence could initiate a new round of civil war. If the civil war ends all over Afghanistan, the only guarantee for the durability of peace and stability there will be the formation of a national reconciliation government. This will have to consist of the political groups representing all the ethnic and religious groups in Afghanistan, otherwise the resumption of civil war will be only a matter of time. It is not certain whether the Afghan interim government will be capable of preparing the ground for the creation of such a government, although it has been mandated to work toward that end.

In Central Asia, it is also feasible to eliminate another source of war and instability. As mentioned before, unrealistic and vague borders between the CA countries have been a source of dispute between and among them. Owing to the fragility of the situation, future disputes could well develop into efforts for a military settlement of disagreements. Major military conflicts will probably take place unless all the CA countries agree on the existing borders or accept a formula for their redrawing. This is not an easy task to undertake, but it is certainly a necessity. In 2001, limited efforts by Uzbekistan and Kazakhstan to settle some of their numerous border disputes through negotiations and trading of lands have indicated the possibility of a peaceful settlement for such disputes. Yet the prospect of a comprehensive agreement between and among all the CA countries on their borders is not, in the foreseeable future, very promising. While many of the minor disputes could be settled fairly easily, the existence of other sources of mistrust and discontent between these countries will probably erode their interest in bilateral and/or multilateral negotiations and agreements over borders. Willingness to make compromise and flexibility—two essential components for negotiations—simply do not exist in most CA governments, which are dissatisfied with each other over a long list of issues. Consequently, border disputes could well develop into major bilateral or multilateral conflicts capable of escalating into military confrontations.

In the Caucasus, the threat of the expansion of war and extremism from Chechnya is real. The region itself is fragile because of its hosting a range of destabilizing forces. The continuation of the Chechen war and the possibility of its expansion to other parts of the Northern Caucasus neighboring Georgia and Azerbaijan reveal the depth of the threat. This scenario should also alarm the Caucasians about the high price they will have to pay if they become indifferent to the ongoing war along their borders with Russia. In practice, there is little they can do to stop that war, which is an internal Russian affair despite its threatening potential for the Caucasus. Yet they should support any future efforts to find a peaceful settlement to the Chechen conflict and to end the civil war in the Northern Caucasus. The absence of any interest in the Russian government in finding a peaceful solution to the military conflict does not leave much hope for its end in the foreseeable future. The current low-key war of attrition will likely continue in the near future, and it could escalate into a more extensive civil war. Hence, the possibility of its expansion to the Caucasus will remain.

In the short run, the prospect for peace is not very great for the countries of the Caucasus and Central Asia. Many influences have paved the way for the rise of wars in different forms, ranging from civil wars to regional wars. The situation is ripe, and will remain so, for instability and war for a predictably long period of time. Only a drastic change in the state of affairs in the two regions could remove the possibility of such destructive developments, which is a highly unrealistic scenario in the near future. The outbreak of any type of military conflict for any length of time will be disastrous for the Caucasians and Central Asians, who have experienced sharp declines in their living standards since independence. Their limited resources and insignificant foreign assistance have prolonged the transitional period from the old Soviet social and economic system to a form of free-enterprise economy with its corresponding social system. Apart from the tragic cost of any military conflict in human lives, such an event will deplete their scarce resources and perpetuate the existing agonizing limbo between the two economic and social systems. In the absence of adequate resources to complete the already long transitional process, this limbo may well become their own economic and social system for an unpredictable period of time.

The impact of war and instability in the Caucasus or Central Asia will not be confined to the countries immediately affected. Any local conflict could escalate and expand to its neighboring countries, only to destabilize its entire respective region. Furthermore, certain countries with stakes in the stability of Central Asia and/or the Caucasus could well be dragged into such a conflict, intentionally or unintentionally. Regardless of the form or extent of their intervention in a future major war, the sheer act of intervention could further escalate the war, increase the human suffering, and plant the seeds for its further escalation. Needless to say, this could only further contribute to the devastation of all parties involved and especially of the "hosting" CA or Caucasian countries. In fact, certain factors could even kindle a military confrontation between and among the five regional and nonregional states with long-term interests in Central Asia and the Caucasus. This scenario could potentially destabilize large parts of Asia and Europe. The geographical location of the two regions as a link between Asia and Europe—shared to different extents by Iran, Turkey, and Russia—creates a "natural" geographical context for the expansion of any regional war involving those states to other parts of Asia and Europe. Added to this, Iran, China, Turkey, Russia, and the United States all have ties and influence in parts of Asia and Europe. They are also members of regional organizations such as the Economic Cooperation Organization (Iran and Turkey) or military organizations such as NATO (Turkey and the United States). These geographical, political, economic and military ties could help expand any conflict in which they are involved.

For all the reasons mentioned, war and instability in the countries of the Caucasus and Central Asia will be bad news for a great number of countries, near or far. It is therefore in the interest of all the potential parties to any future military conflict in the two regions to avoid actions that could instigate it. They should also refrain from acts that could unnecessarily escalate such conflicts should they occur. On the contrary, they should employ all their powers to contain and to end such conflicts. Perhaps more importantly than any of these, they should all contribute to the efforts of the Caucasian and CA countries to revitalize their economies and resolve their disputes with their neighboring states or within their own national boundaries. One should hope that, for the sake of peace and stability, Iran, China, Turkey, Russia, and the United States will find enough incentives to become contributing partners to a process of economic growth and peaceful resolution of conflicts in the Caucasus and Central Asia. Otherwise, there is little doubt that the current pace of events in the two regions is heading toward a period of war and instability, with a devastating result for the exhausted Caucasian and CA countries. This development will contain a great potential for escalation, with severe implications for the security of many other countries in Asia and Europe.

Bibliography

Books

Akiner, Shirin. "A Social and Political Reorganization." In *Central Asia: Transition from Pre-Colonial to Post-Colonial Society, Post-Soviet Central Asia.* London: Tauris Academic Studies, 1998.

d'Encausse, Helene Carrere. "Civil War and New Governments." In *Central Asia: 120 Years of Russian Rule*, ed. Edward Allworth. Durham, NC: Duke University Press, 1989, pp. 224–253.

d'Encausse, Helene Carrere. "The Fall of the Czarist Empire." In *Central Asia: 120 Years of Russian Rule*, ed. Edward Allworth. Durham, NC: Duke University Press, 1989, pp. 207–223.

Eklof, Ben. *Soviet Briefing: Gorbachev and the Reform Period.* Boulder, IN: Westview Press, 1989.

Falkingham, Jane, Jeni Klugman, Sheila Marine, and John Micklewright. "Household Welfare in Central Asia: An Introduction to the Issues." In *Household Welfare in Central Asia*, ed. Jane Falkingham, Jeni Klugman, Sheila Marine, and John Micklewright. London: Macmillan, 1997, pp. 1–10.

Hosking, Geoffrey. *A History of the Soviet Union.* London: Fontana Press, 1985.

Klugman, Jeni, and George Schrieber. "A Survey of Health Reform in Central Asia." In *Implementing Health Sector Reform in Central Asia: Paper from a Health Policy Seminar Held in Ashgabat, Turkmenistan, June 1996*, ed. Zuzana Feachem, Martin Hensher and Laura Rose. Washington, D.C.: The World Bank, 1999.

Olcott, Martha Brill. "Central Asia's Political Crisis." In *Russia's Muslim Frontier*, ed. Dale F. Eickelman. Bloomington, IN: Indiana University Press, 1993.

Passdarmachian, Herand. *History of Armenia*. Tehran: Zarrin, 1999.

Peimani, Hooman. *The Caspian Pipeline Dilemma: Political Games and Economic Losses*. Westport, CT: Praeger, 2001.

Peimani, Hooman. *Iran and the United States: The Rise of the West Asian Regional Grouping*. Westport, CT: Praeger, 1999.

Peimani, Hooman. *Regional Security and the Future of Central Asia: The Competition of Iran, Turkey, and Russia*. Westport, CT: Praeger, 1998.

Riasanovsky, Nicholas V. A *History of Russia*, 4th ed. New York: Oxford University Press, 1984.

Shuval, Judith T., and Judith H. Bernstein, eds. *Immigrant Physicians: Former Soviet Doctors in Israel, Canada, and the United States*. Westport, CT: Praeger, 1997.

Journal Articles

Amirahmadian, Bahram. "The Trend of Developments in the Karabakh Crisis." *Majelieh-e Motaellat-e Asyaie Markazi va Ghafghaz [Central Asia and the Caucasus Review]* (Tehran), 28 (Winter 2000): 27–50.

Arfaei, Alieh. "Nagorno Karabakh's Sad Case." *Majelieh-e Motaellat-e Asyaie Markazi va Ghafghaz [Central Asia and the Caucasus Review]* (Tehran), 1, No. 2 (Autumn 1992): 153–206.

Attaie, Farhad. "A Retrospective Glance at the History and the Current Situation of the Central Asian Republics." *Majelieh-e Motaellat-e Asyaie Markazi va Ghafghaz [Central Asia and the Caucasus Review]* (Tehran), 1, No. 3 (Winter 1993): 151–164.

"Azerbaijan." *Eurasian File* (Ankara), 133 (August 2000): 3–4.

"Azerbaijan to Increase Military Spending." Radio Free Europe/Radio Liberty [REF/RL], 9 March 2001.

Bayat, Kaveh. "A Look at the Relations of Iran with the First Armenian Republic, 1918–1921." *Majelieh-e Motaellat-e Asyaie Markazi va Ghafghaz [Central Asia and the Caucasus Review* (Tehran), 25 (Spring 1999): 125–132.

Blackwill, Robert D., Rodric Braithwaite, and Akihiko Tanaka. "Russia's National Interests." *Majelieh-e Motaellat-e Asyaie Markazi va Ghafghaz [Central Asia and the Caucasus Review]* (Tehran), 23 (Fall 1998): 47–64.

"Brain Drain in Armenia." Institute for War & Peace Reporting, Caucasus Reporting Service, 10 Jan 2000, 08:44:04 EST.

Calabrese, John. "China's Policy Towards Central Asia: Renewal and Accommodation." *Eurasian Studies* (Ankara), 16 (Autumn–Winter 1999): 75–98.

Dannreuther, Roland. "Creating New States in Central Asia." *Adelphi Paper,* 288 (March 1994): 2–82.

Dannreuther, Roland. "Russia, Central Asia and the Persian Gulf." *Survival,* 35 (4) (Winter 1993–94): 92–112.

de Nevers, Renee. "Russia's Strategic Renovation." *Adelphi Paper, 289* (July 1994): 5–81.

Document Publishing Unit. "A Glance at the History of the Northeastern Borders (From Sarakhs to Caspian)—Part One." *Majelieh-e Motaellat-e Asyaie Markazi va Ghafghaz* [*Central Asia and the Caucasus Review*] (Tehran) 1, No. 1 (Summer 1992): 231–242.

Document Publishing Unit. "A Glance at the History of the Northeastern Borders (From Sarakhs to Caspian)—Part Two." *Majelieh-e Motaellat-e Asyaie Markazi va Ghafghaz* [*Central Asia and the Caucasus Review*] (Tehran), 1, No. 2 (Autumn 1992): 259–280.

"Economic Indicators in Azerbaijan." *Eurasian File* (Ankara), 139 (February 2001): 2.

"Economic Outlooks and Prospects: Natural Resources." *DEIK Bulletin-Uzbekistan* (Istanbul), (April 1993): 2.

Economist Intelligence Unit. *Kazakhstan: Country Profile 1998*–99. London: Economist Intelligence Unit, 1998.

Economist Intelligence Unit. *Kyrgyz Republic-Tajikistan: Country Report–4th Quarter 1998.* The Economist Intelligence Unit, 1998.

"The Economy." *DEIK Bulletin-Kyrgyzstan* (Istanbul), (June 1994): 2.

"The Economy: Energy." *DEIK Bulletin-Kyrgyzstan* (Istanbul), (June 1994): 2.

"Europe: The End of an Empire." *Strategic Survey 1991–1992* (May 2000): 27–36.

Faghani, Hojatolah. "The Eastward Expansion of NATO: A Review of Georgia's Position." *Majelieh-e Motaellat-e Asyaie Markazi va Ghafghaz* [*Central Asia and the Caucasus Review*] (Tehran), 26 (Summer 1999): 19–30.

Farzin-nia, Ziba. "The Emergence of the Taliban on the Afghan Scene." *Majelieh-e Motaellat-e Asyaie Markazi va Ghafghaz* [*Central Asia and the Caucasus Review*] (Tehran), 23 (Fall 1998): 15–28.

Fergus, Michael. "The Aral Sea Environmental Crisis: Problems and a Way Forward." *Asian Affairs,* 30, No. 1 (February 1999): 35–44.

"General Economic Outlooks and Prospects." *DEIK Bulletin-Kyrgyzstan* (Istanbul), (April 1993): 2.

Hiro, Dilip. "A Failed Revolt." *Middle East International,* 25 December 1998, 19.

Hiro, Dilip. "A Bomb Blast in Tashkent." *Middle East International*, 12 March 1999, 16.

"Increasing the Quality of Kyrgyz Tobacco." *Eurasian File* (Ankara), 138 (January 2001): 12.

Institute for War & Peace Reporting. Caucasus Reporting Service. No. 15b, Mon, 24 Jan 2000, 07:24:20 EST.

Institute for War & Peace Reporting. Caucasus Reporting Service. *TransCaucasus: A Chronology*, 9, No. 6 (9 June 2000).

Ivanov, A.M. "Armenia's Economic Co-operation with Russia." *Majelieh-e Motaellat-e Asyaie Markazi va Ghafghaz [Central Asia and the Caucasus Review]* (Tehran), 28 (Winter 2000), 128.

Klatt, Martin. "Russians in the 'Near Abroad.'" *REF/RL Research Report*, 3, No. 32 (19 August 1994): 33–44.

"Kyrgyz Parliament Calls on President to Disavow Border Accord." REF/RL, 16 June 2001.

Lelyveld, Michael. "Azerbaijan: Caspian Region Faces Fuel Shortages." REF/RL, 3 February 2000, 1 (internet text).

Maleki, Gassem Maleki, "The Aral Sea: An Environmental Crisis." *Majelieh-e Motaellat-e Asyaie Markazi va Ghafghaz [Central Asia and the Caucasus Review]* (Tehran), 26 (Summer 1999): 53–66.

McMahon, Robert. "Georgia: UN Envoy Hopes Abkhaz Status Talks Follow Yalta Success." RFE/RL, 22 March 2001.

"Meeting Between Armenian, Azerbaijani Presidents Postponed." REF/RL, 29 May 2001.

"Newsline." REF/RL, 29 May 2001.

"Newsline." REF/RL, 13 June 2000.

"Newsline." REF/RL, 4 September 2000.

Nossrat, Nassrin. "The Economic Situation of the Republic of Uzbekistan." *Majelieh-e Motaellat-e Asyaie Markazi va Ghafghaz [Central Asia and the Caucasus Review]* (Tehran), 1, No. 4 (Spring 1993): 237–252.

Omidvarniya, Mohammad Javad. "A Review of the Natural Geography of the Xinjiang Uyghur Autonomous Region." *Majelieh-e Motaellat-e Asyaie Markazi va Ghafghaz [Central Asia and the Caucasus Review]* (Tehran), 1, No. 2 (Summer 1993): 131–150.

Pannier, Bruce. "Central Asia: Border Dispute between Uzbekistan and Kyrgyzstan Risks Triggering Conflict." REF/RL, 8 March 1999.

Pannier, Bruce. "Central Asia: Shanghai Cooperation Organisation Ends Summit." REF/RL, 15 June 2001.

Pannier, Bruce. "Uzbekistan: Human Rights Watch Calls Tashkent Trials Unfair." REF/RL, 4 June 2001.

Peimani, Hooman. "Has the Taliban Regime Eradicated Opium Production?" *Central Asia–Caucasus Analyst* (11 April 2001).

Peuch, Jean-Christophe. "Caucasus: Georgia Sees Future in Regional Co-operation." REF/RL, 11 May 2001.

Peuch, Jean-Christophe. "Georgia: Corruption Seen as the 'Norm.'" REF/RL, 10 May 2001.

Peuch, Jean-Christophe. "Georgia: Little Hope Seen for Abkhaz Peace Process." REF/RL, 4 May 2001.

Ratter, Igor. "Will Central Asia Explode?" *Majelieh-e Motaellat-e Asyaie Markazi va Ghafghaz* [*Central Asia and the Caucasus Review*] (Tehran), 2, No. 1 (Summer 1993): 195–204.

Saghafi-Ameri, Nasser. "Editorial Note." *Majelieh-e Motaellat-e Asyaie Markazi va Ghafghaz* [*Central Asia and the Caucasus Review*] (Tehran), 28 (Winter 2000): 7–10.

Salmasi-zadeh, Mohammad. "A Glance at the Historical Geography of Georgia: From the First Century to the End of the 10th Century." *Majelieh-e Motaellat-e Asyaie Markazi va Ghafghaz* [*Central Asia and the Caucasus Review*] (Tehran), 28 (Winter 2000): 105–126.

Sarir, Mohammad, and Narsi Ghorban. "Developments of the Oil Industry in Azerbaijan and Its Regional and International Positions." *Majelieh-e Motaellat-e Asyaie Markazi va Ghafghaz* [*Central Asia and the Caucasus Review*] (Tehran), 2, No. 1 (Summer 1993): 169–184.

Shahabi, Sohrab. "A General View of the Economic Conditions of Central Asian Republics." *Majelieh-e Motaellat-e Asyaie Markazi va Ghafghaz* [*Central Asia and the Caucasus Review*] (Tehran), 1, No. 2 (Autumn 1992): 122–123.

Shaldiz, Valery. " The Ossetian Crisis in Georgia." *Majelieh-e Motaellat-e Asyaie Markazi va Ghafghaz* [*Central Asia and the Caucasus Review*] (Tehran), 2, No. 1 (Summer 1993): 163–168.

Sharmanov, Almaz. "Anaemia in Central Asia: Demographic and Health Survey Experience." *Food and Nutrition Bulletin*, 19, No. 4 (1998): 307–318.

Sozar, Subelian. "Turning Over a New Leaf in Tbilisi?" Institute for War & Peace Reporting, Caucasus Reporting Service, 10 Jan 2000, 08:44:04 EST.

Spoor, Max. "The Aral Sea Basin Crisis: Transition and Environment in Former Soviet Central Asia." *Development and Change*, 29 (3) (July 1998): 409–435.

Takmil Homayun, Naser. "A Glance at Karabakh in Iran's History." *Majelieh-e Motaellat-e Asyaie Markazi va Ghafghaz [Central Asia and the Caucasus Review]* (Tehran), 2, No. 1 (Summer 1993): 59–98.

"Uighur Activist Found Murdered in Kazakhstan." REF/RL, 13 June 2001.

"Uzbekistan." *Eurasian File* (Ankara), 133 (August 2000): 5.

Vahidi, Musa al-Reza. "Russia and the Crisis in the Northern Caucasus." *Majelieh-e Motaellat-e Asyaie Markazi va Ghafghaz [Central Asia and the Caucasus Review]* (Tehran), 28 (Winter 2000): 11–26.

Zakareishvili, Paata. "An Open Wound." Institute for War & Peace Reporting, Caucasus Reporting Service, No. 15b, 24 January 2000.

Magazine and Newspaper Articles

"Central Asia: The Shrinking Hordes." *The Economist*, 3 April 1999, 53.

"Glimpse of a Troubled Land." *The Economist*, 1 May 1999, 59.

Peimani, Hooman. "Drug-Trafficking in the Ferghana Valley and Instability in Central Asia." *The Times of Central Asia* (Bishkek), 2 November 2000.

"Signs of Discontent." *The Times of Central Asia* (Bishkek), 14 October 2000, 8.

Other Sources

CNN News. European Edition, 9 p.m., 25 May 2001.

Department of Economic and Social Affairs. *World Economic and Social Survey 2000.* New York: United Nations, 2000.

Independent Republic of Kazakhstan: Report of a UNICEF/WHO Collaborative Mission with the Participation of UNDP, UNFPA, and WFP, Alma Ata, Kazakhstan, 17–26 February 1992.

The Invisible Emergency: A Crisis of Children and Women in Tajikistan. Report of a UNICEF/WHO Collaborative Mission with the Participation of UNDP, UNFPA, and WFP (17–21 February 1992).

Koopman, Jeanne. *Gender Issues in Farm Restructuring in Uzbekistan and Kyrgyzstan: Implications for the BASIS Research Program.* Washington, D.C.: International Research on Women and BASIS Project, Land Tenure Center, April 1998.

The Looming Crisis of Children and Women in Kyrgyzstan. Report of a UNICEF/WHO Collaborative Mission with the Participation of UNDP, UNFPA, and WFP, 21–26 February 1992 (17 March 1992).

Republic of Uzbekistan. Report of a UNICEF/WHO Collaborative Mission with the Participation of UNDP, UNFPA, and WFP (21 February to 2 March 1992), Tashkent, Uzbekistan, 16 March 1992, 4.

Seeds of Change: Survival in the Pamirs. Video produced by the Aga Khan Foundation, 1995.

Seminar Held in Ashgabat, Turkmenistan, June 1996, ed. Zuzana Feachem, Martin Hensher, and Laura Rose. Washington, D.C.: The World Bank, 1999, p. 22.

"Tajikistan: Introductory Survey." In *The Europa World Year Book 1994.* London: Europa Publications, 1994, p. 2752.

To Beijing and Beyond: The Gender Gap in Eastern Europe and the Commonwealth of Independent States (CIS) and the Baltic States—NGO Forum, Beijing. New York: UNDP, 1995.

UNDP, *Development Cooperation: Uzbekistan.* New York: UNDP, June 1995.

UNDP, *Human Development Report 1999.* New York: Oxford University Press, 1999.

UNDP, *Human Development Report 2000.* New York: Oxford University Press, 2000.

WHO Regional Office for Europe. *Highlight on Women's Health: Tajikistan.* Copenhagen, 1994.

The World Bank. *World Developmental Indicators 1997.* Washington, D.C.: The World Bank, 1997.

The World Bank. *World Developmental Indicators 1998.* Washington, D.C.: The World Bank, 1998.

The World Bank. *World Developmental Indicators 1999.* Washington, D.C.: The World Bank, 1999.

The World Bank. *World Developmental Indicators 2000.* Washington, D.C.: The World Bank, 2000.

Women and Gender in Countries in Transition: A UNICEF Perspective. New York: UNICEF, 1995.

Index

ABOUT THE AUTHOR

Hooman Peimani works as an independent consultant with international organizations in Geneva, Switzerland, and does research in International Relations. His earlier writing has centered on the Persian Gulf, the Caucasus, Central Asia, and the Indian subcontinent. His recent publications include *The Caspian Pipeline Dilemma: Political Games and Economic Losses* (Praeger, 2001); *Nuclear Proliferation in the Indian Subcontinent: The Self-Exhausting "Superpowers" and Emerging Alliances* (Praeger, 2000); *Iran and the United States: The Rise of the West Asian Regional Grouping* (Praeger, 1999); and *Regional Security and the Future of Central Asia: The Competition of Iran, Turkey, and Russia* (Praeger, 1998).